Introduction to
DB2 Programming

ISBN	AUTHOR	TITLE
0-07-056578-3	Sherman	*The CD-ROM Handbook*
0-07-039006-1	Lusardi	*Database Experts' Guide to SQL*
0-07-039002-9	(softcover)	
0-07-016609-6	DeVita	*Database Experts' Guide to FOCUS*
0-07-016604-8	(softcover)	
0-07-036488-5	Larson	*Database Experts' Guide to Database 2*
0-07-023267-9	(softcover)	
0-07-000474-9	Adrian	*The Workstation Data Link*
0-07-057336-0	Simpson, Casey	*Developing Effective User Documentation*
0-07-007248-5	Brathwaite	*Analysis, Design, and Implementation of Data Dictionaries*
0-07-035119-8	Knightson	*Standards for Open Systems Interconnection*
0-07-044938-4	McClain	*VM and Departmental Computing*
0-07-044939-2	(softcover)	
0-07-046302-6	Nemzow	*Keeping the Link*
0-07-038006-6	Lipton	*User Guide to FOCUS*
0-07-003355-2	Baker	*C-Tools for Scientists and Engineers*
0-07-057296-8	Simon	*How to Be a Successful Computer Consultant*
0-07-052061-5	Rhee	*Error Correction Coding Theory*
0-07-016188-7	Dayton (Ranade, Ed.)	*Integrating Digital Services*
0-07-002673-4	Azevedo (Ranade Series)	*ISPF: The Strategic Dialog Manager*
0-07-050054-1	Piggott (Ranade Series)	*CICS: A Practical Guide to System Fine Tuning*
0-07-043152-3	Morgan, McGilton	*Introducing UNIX™ System V*
0-07-050686-8	Prasad (Ranade Series)	*IBM Mainframes*
0-07-065087-X	Towner (Ranade Series)	*IDMS/R Cookbook*
0-07-062879-3	Tare (hardcover)	*UNIX™ Utilities*
0-07-062884-X	Tare (softcover)	*UNIX™ Utilities*
0-07-045001-3	McGilton, Morgan	*Introducing the UNIX™ System*
0-07-062295-7	Su	*Database Computers*
0-07-041920-5	Milenkovic	*Operating Systems Concepts and Design*
0-07-010829-3	Ceri, Pelagotti	*Distributed Databases*

For more information about other McGraw-Hill materials, call 1-800-2-MCGRAW in the United States. In other countries, call your nearest McGraw-Hill office.

Introduction to DB2 Programming

Viet G. Tran

McGraw-Hill Publishing Company

New York   St. Louis   San Francisco   Auckland   Bogotá
Caracas   Colorado Springs   Hamburg   Lisbon
London   Madrid   Mexico   Milan   Montreal
New Delhi   Oklahoma City   Panama   Paris
San Juan   São Paulo   Singapore
Sydney   Tokyo   Toronto

To my parents, Tam Tran and Minh Tran, who gave me life and brought me up in this world.

To my wife, Thuy, and my children, Jacqueline and Joanne.

Library of Congress Cataloging-in-Publication Data

Tran, Viet G.
　　Introduction to DB2 programming / Viet G. Tran.
　　　　p.　cm.
　　Includes index.
　　ISBN 0-07-065120-5
　　1. Data base management.　2. IBM Database 2 (Computer system)
I. Title.
QA76.9.D3T69　1989　　　　　　　　　　　　　　　88-31874
　　　　　　　　　　　　　　　　　　　　　　　　　　　CIP

1234567890　DOC/DOC　895432109

ISBN 0-07-065120-5

The editors for this book were Theron Shreve and Nancy Young, the designer was Naomi Auerbach, and the production supervisor was Dianne L. Walber. This book was set in Century Schoolbook. It was composed by the McGraw-Hill Publishing Company Professional & Reference Division composition unit.

Printed and bound by R. R. Donnelley & Sons Company.

For more information about other McGraw-Hill materials, call 1-800-2-MCGRAW in the United States. In other countries, call your nearest McGraw-Hill office.

Contents

Preface

Database techniques have evolved greatly with the fast-growing computer industry. As more people rely on database management systems (DBMS), different sophisticated DBMS that use various database models become available.

This book deals mainly with the application programming and query techniques that can be used in an IBM Database2 database environment because Database2 can be used either as an embedded language or an ad hoc query language. Database2 is the latest DBMS supplied by IBM. It is a relational database management system designed to use state-of-the-art software and hardware technology.

This book can be used by application programmers and others who want to learn IBM Database2 or other SQL-based DBMS. It covers the basic syntax and techniques and shows how to use them in practical situations.

Database design is not discussed in this book. Although this topic is extremely important in deciding what data elements should be grouped together in a database, it is covered separately in other books dealing specifically with database design techniques.

This book assumes no prior knowledge of Database2 or any other DBMS. However for technical users, some knowledge of the IBM operating systems that support Database2 and of the IBM virtual storage access method (VSAM) is helpful but not necessary.

Chapter 1 introduces the IBM Database2, its operating environments, and its main features. Chapter 2 introduces Database2 terminology, its structure, and the language that operates in its environment. These two chapters can be omitted by readers who have some basic knowledge about IBM Database2. Chapter 3 shows how to describe a database to DATABASE2. Chapters 4, 5, and 6 introduce the concept of database retrieval and database maintenance. Chapter 7 introduces the advanced features of Database2, which include secondary indexing and views. Chapter 8 is for technical users; it covers topics such as table space and access methods. Chapter 9 covers Dynamic SQL, which is an important feature of Database 2. Chapter

10 gives some tips on performance when using Database2, an overview of all the DB2 utilities, and the query management facility (QMF).

This book also has four appendixes: Appendix A is a full description of the Database 2 catalog, Appendix B contains all the examples written in PL/I, Appendix C lists all the Database2 allowable data types and their equivalents in COBOL and PL/I languages, and Appendix D lists all the Database2 reserved words.

In order to illustrate the main features of Database2, we use a database designed for a fictitious hospital named CARING. All the examples presented in this book are written in COBOL.

Viet Tran

Acknowledgments

The author is grateful for all those who assisted in reviewing the manuscript and who contributed useful suggestions and to IBM corporation for permission to use some of their copyrighted material. The following materials are printed with permission from IBM publications:

Figure 1.1 is printed from publication SC26-4077-2, copyrighted in 1982, 1984, and 1986.

Figure 3.7 is printed with modification from publication SC26-4081-2, copyrighted in 1983, 1984, and 1986.

Appendixes A and D are printed from publication SC26-4078-2, copyrighted in 1983, 1984, and 1986.

What Is Database2?

The purpose of this book is to show you the programming techniques that can be used in an IBM Database2 (DB2) environment. This book can also be used as a handy reference for anyone who needs to know about DB2 or Structured Query Language/Data System (SQL/DS), which is the DB2 version that runs under DOS/VSE and VM. In this chapter, we'll discuss some of the main purposes and objectives of DB2.

1.1 The Objectives of DB2

Most database management systems' objectives are to increase data independence, reduce data redundancy, and provide data communications facilities. However, as more companies rely on database management systems (DBMS) to record their vital information, new DBMS are required to increase productivity and for ease of use and flexibility.

We'll see that DB2 increases productivity by using a high-level language that is very easy to learn and also that requests for data are independent of physical data organization. DB2 databases can be defined and maintained very quickly. As more information gets stored in the computer, a wider range of users with different levels of data processing skills need to process this information. Because of its simplicity, application programs using DB2 can be developed very rapidly.

Companies tend to grow with their data processing needs and a great deal of money is usually invested in their existing systems; hence any new system must work efficiently with existing systems.

DB2 provides this flexibility by having different attachment facilities for other subsystems. We'll discuss them in the next section.

1.2 DB2 Operating Environments

The IBM DB2 is a relational database designed to use state-of-the-art software and hardware technology to meet the requirements of today's changing industries. DB2 can run in an IBM MVS/XA (Multiple Virtual Storage/Extended Architecture), in an IBM MVS/370 environment, or in any later IBM MVS environment (see Figure 1.1).

1.3 The Main Features of IBM DB2

DB2 runs as a subsystem in an MVS environment. Attachment facilities are provided with DB2 to allow interfacing with other IBM MVS subsystems (TSO, IMS/VS, and CICS/OS/VS) to coordinate resource commitment. DB2 has no data communication capabilities of its own, but it can be accessed through transaction managers. Since DB2 works with IMS/VS and CICS/OS/VS transaction managers, its operation is not affected even when the transaction managers stop or fail.

1.3.1 TSO attachment facility

The time-sharing option (TSO) is a system that allows a number of users to use the facilities of a computer concurrently at a terminal in a conversational manner. The users request that work be done by typing TSO commands on a terminal. The system performs the work and sends messages back to the terminal. With the TSO attachment facil-

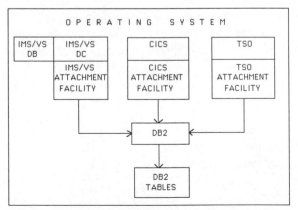

Fig. 1.1 DB2 operating environment.

ity, the users can access DB2 databases interactively through a TSO session or by running a batch TSO job in background.

1.3.2 IMS/VS attachment facility

Information Management System/Virtual Storage (IMS/VS) is a database and data communication (DB/DC) system. IMS/VS provides the facilities to create and maintain hierarchical databases. It also provides the data communication facilities that allow online execution of application programs accessing IMS/VS databases. With this attachment, requests to access DB2 databases are received from IMS/VS subsystems. Only IMS/VS data communications programs are able to access DB2; IMS/VS provides the data communication services and DB2 provides the database services. The following data communications programs are allowed to access DB2:

Batch message processing (BMP)

Message processing program (MPP)

Fast path program

1.3.3 CICS/OS/VS attachment facility

Customer Information Control System/Virtual Storage (CICS/VS) is a data communication system that provides an environment for customized online information processing systems (i.e., personnel system, library system, etc.). In order to gain access to the CICS facilities, application programs must contain embedded CICS command statements. CICS/OS/VS is the CICS/VS version that runs under the OS/MVS operating system. With the CICS/OS/VS is the CICS/VS version that runs under the OS/MVS operating system. With the attachment facility, DB2 databases can be accessed by CICS application programs with full data integrity and recoverability. Connection between DB2 and CICS can be established automatically or at any time after DB2 has started.

2

DB2 Terminology

The main purpose of this chapter is to introduce a series of terms that we will need to understand in a DB2 environment. If we're familiar with other relational database management systems, we will find that some of them are similar. In order to facilitate this task, we will go through all the steps necessary to define and use a sample database constructed for a fictitious hospital. The sample applications are used to keep track of information about the Caring Hospital. The database designed and the sample applications used for it are not meant to solve any problems in the real world but rather to illustrate the capabilities of the IBM DB2 database management system.

2.1 The Relational Database

The first concept that we'll introduce is that of "table structure." In a relational database, each file (a file is called a "relation" in relational terminology) consists of a subset of identically formatted records. The records of a relation are called "tuples." Each field or component of a tuple belongs to a different set of values or a domain which describes a particular characteristic about that tuple. To better understand relations, it helps to represent them as tables, where a table consists of a set of columns and some number of rows. We can see that each row corresponds to a tuple and each column is a component. Each column possesses a unique name, and different tables can have columns with the same names. A basic table of the Caring Hospital database is shown in Figure 2.1.

Example 2.1   In Figure 2.1 we see a table named PATIENT whose attributes or column names are PATNAME, PATNO, ADDRESS, BIRTHDATE, SEX, and SSNUM. For example, the following is a row, or tuple, that belongs to the PATIENT table:

```
(smith,0001,123 first street        ,400320,m,111001111)
```

PATNAME	PATNO	ADDRESS	BIRTHDATE	SEX	SSNUM
SMITH	0001	123 FIRST STREET	400320	M	111001111
DOE	0010	225 WILHIRE BLVD	550912	M	221002222
JACKSON	0005	654 SOTO STREET	541205	F	330113323
ADAMS	0003	5674 SUNSET STREET	400320	M	442134366
BROWN	0028	12 WILLOW STREET	640213	F	343350945
JOHNSON	0020	9534 VALLEY BLVD	330814	M	348650973
PARKER	0017	7655 GRAND AVENUE	781112	F	689545853
LEE	0042	7462 SANTA MONICA	450530	M	788575443

Fig. 2.1   Sample of a DB2 table (PATIENT relation or table).

The columns in a table are in a specified order when we define the table to DB2, but the rows do not have to be in any special order. Let's explore the Caring database further by looking at different tables and relations.

Figure 2.2 shows the Physician table with column names PHYNAME, PHYNO, DEPARTMENT, HIREDATE, and SALARY. Figure 2.3 shows the Visit table with column names IDNO, SEQUN, MDNO, ADDATE, DSDATE, and DIAGNOSIS. Of course, we are free to create tables with any sets of columns and to put any interpretation on the rows. But notice that in a table, the following relationship is always true for any row that belongs to table T. Table T has m columns called C1, C2,...,Cm and row r of table T has components c1, c2,...,cm. For any component k between 1 and m, ck always belongs to the column Ck. In other words, all the rows in a table are related by the relationship defined in that table.

Example 2.2   Take a row from the Physician table in Figure 2.2:

```
(stern,345,general medicine,750312,43720)
```

We can see that "stern" belongs to column PHYNAME, "345" belongs to column PHYNO, etc. In other words, the components of a row are related to each other in the table or relation PHYSICIAN.

2.1.1   DB2 table structure

The columns in each table are related to each other by an underlying relationship. The PATIENT table describes attributes about each pa-

PHYNAME	PHYNO	DEPARTMENT	HIREDATE	SALARY
STERN	345	GENERAL MEDICINE	750312	43720
MITCHUM	867	OBSTETRICS	661211	58760
MILLER	234	DERMATOLOGY	670423	59670
THOMPSON	432	NEUROLOGY	760322	76540
BURTON	479	CARDIOLOGY	470506	85786
JONES	916	PEDIATRICS	731205	49658
STEIN	612	GENERAL MEDICINE	801115	43658

Fig. 2.2   Physician table.

IDNO	SEQUN	MDNO	ADDATE	DSDATE	DIAGNOSIS
0001	001	234	850810	850810	ITCHING
0001	002	612	851020	851020	FLU
0010	001	345	851112	851112	BRONCHITIS
0005	001	867	860110	860110	ABDOMINAL PAIN
0003	001	432	850320	850325	CONCUSSION
0028	001	234	860520	860520	SKIN RASH
0020	001	479	851010	851020	HEART ATTACK
0017	001	916	860210	860210	FLU
0042	001	345	860617	860617	CHEST PAIN

Fig. 2.3   Visit table.

tient. Therefore, patient name (PATNAME), patient number (PATNO), patient address (ADDRESS), patient birth date (BIRTH-DATE), patient sex (SEX), and patient social security number (SSNUM) are facts about a patient. Each row in the PATIENT table describes some characteristics about a patient by having different attribute values.

Example 2.3   The PHYSICIAN table in Figure 2.2 describes facts about each physician such as physician name (PHYNAME), physician ID (PHYNO), physician department (DEPARTMENT), date of employment (HIREDATE), and annual salary (SALARY). In a similar fashion, the VISIT table in Figure 2.3 describes information about each patient visit to the hospital, such as patient identification number (IDNO), sequence number of the visit (SEQUN), ID number of physician who sees the patient for that visit (MDNO), admit date (ADDATE), discharge date (DSDATE), and patient diagnosis (DIAGNOSIS).

No matter what information a table may contain, each table should have one or more columns with a unique value to identify the rows of the table. That column or set of columns is the "primary key" of the table. In the PATIENT table in Figure 2.1, PATNO is the primary key, as shown below:

PATNAME	PATNO	ADDRESS	BIRTHDATE	SEX	SSNUM

<..key.. >

Each patient is assigned a unique identification number the first time he or she comes to the hospital for treatment. Thus each row contains information that belongs to one and only one patient. Of course, we can choose any field in the table to be the primary key as long as it takes on a different value for each row. Since each one of us has a different social security number, let's look at the patient's social security number as a primary key. We can see right away that it is not a very good choice because a patient may or may not have a social security number.

Each physician in the PHYSICIAN table in Figure 2.2 is assigned a unique identification number at the start of employment. Thus, the physician ID (PHYNO) is the primary key in the Physician table, as shown below:

PHYNAME	PHYNO	DEPARTMENT	HIREDATE	SALARY

< ..key... >

The VISIT table in Figure 2.3 describes information about each patient visit. Since each patient could be in the hospital more than once, we use a sequence number (SEQUN) starting with 001 to identify each visit. In order to differentiate each row in the VISIT table, we need to know two things: the patient a particular visit belongs to and the sequence number of the visit. As a result, the primary key in the VISIT table is made of two columns: IDNO and SEQUN:

IDNO	SEQUN	MDNO	ADDATE	DSDATE	DIAGNOSIS

< .....key..... >

As you might expect, the way that the information gets stored in the above tables is the result of our database design. There are a lot of steps to take before deciding which entities are to be grouped in the same table. Database design is beyond the scope of this book, but we will briefly discuss the concept behind the relational database design theory. The whole concept is a set of guidelines called "normal forms" that are designed to prevent update anomalies and data inconsistencies in all the nonkey fields in a table. The process is called "normalization." We will not go into the whole mathematical concept behind the normalization rules, but rather, we will present the guidelines in plain English to make them easier to understand.

Before discussing what the normal forms or normalization rules are, let's see why an unnormalized design might not work. Let's look at a design in which we combine the PATIENT table and the VISIT table into one table with the columns shown in Figure 2.4. We can see right away that there are several problems with this design:

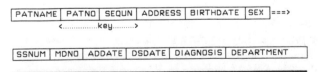

Fig. 2.4 Combined table.

1. The patient address, birth date, sex, and social security number are duplicated in every row in the table. This is a data redundancy problem.

2. If the patient address is updated in only one row, we encounter a data inconsistency problem. Because of the data redundancy problem, we might have different rows showing different addresses for the same patient.

There are four normal forms of tables discussed in most database design books and five in others. The whole theory boils down to a fairly common-sense concept which relies mainly on plain intuition. The following is a brief description of the rules for the first four normal forms of tables. The readers should refer to other books if in-depth understanding about the subject is required.

1. Each table must contain only a fixed number of columns. In other words, each row in a table must have the same number of components. Variable-length records or rows do not exist in relational database theory.

2. Any nonkey field in a table must describe a fact about the whole key. The key in the combined table in Figure 2.4 consists of SEQUN and PATNO together. The patient address (ADDRESS) depends only on the value of the first part of the key (PATNO) but not of the whole key.

3. Any nonkey field in a table can only describe a fact about the key. In Figure 2.4 DEPARTMENT is a fact about the physician (MDNO) but not about the key, which is PATNO and SEQUN.

4. No row in a table should contain two or more independent multi-valued facts about an entity (an entity is something which we want information about, such as patients and visits).

Consider facts about patients, insurance, and dependents, where a patient may have several insurance carriers and have several dependents. In fact, there are two relationships, one between patients and insurance and one between patients and dependents. We should have a separate table for each relationship instead of combining them into one. Figure 2.5a and b shows samples of unnormalized and normalized tables.

After looking at the examples in the figures, readers should realize that there are some performance trade-offs between unnormalized tables and normalized ones. Normalized tables tend to put more overhead on retrieval, since data which reside in one row from an unnormalized design may have to be retrieved from multiple rows in the normalized form. When dealing with a large number of tables that

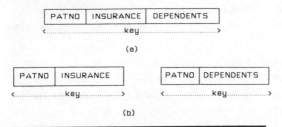

Fig. 2.5 (a) Table that violates the fourth normal form rule and (b) tables in fourth normal form.

are fully normalized, data retrieval can be very costly. Thus, a fully normalized design is not absolutely necessary when actual performance requirements are taken into account.

2.1.2 Relationships among tables

To illustrate the relationships among the tables, let's look at the tables in Figures 2.1, 2.2, 2.3, and two new tables called DEPARTMENT and INSURANCE. The DEPARTMENT table contains information about departments in the hospital and the INSURANCE table contains information about different insurance companies. Figure 2.6 shows some of the relationships that may exist among the tables. They are:

1. Each patient can have many visits to the hospital and many visits can belong to a single patient. Thus a relationship which has one value in one direction and several values in the other is a one-to-many or many-to-one relationship. The relationship HAS is a one-to-many relationship from PATIENT to VISIT.

2. The relationship CARRIES between PATIENT and INSURANCE is a many-to-many relationship in the sense that a PATIENT may have more than one insurance carrier and more than one PA-

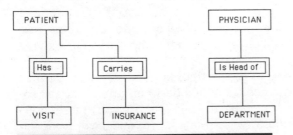

Fig. 2.6 Sample relationship diagram for Caring Hospital database.

TIENT can have the same number of insurance carriers. In other words, a relationship that has several values in both directions is a many-to-many relationship.

3. The relationship IS HEAD OF is a one-to-one relationship between PHYSICIAN and DEPARTMENT because a physician is head of a department and a department can only have one department head. A one-to-one relationship is a relationship that has one value in both directions.

We can see that the relationships can be:

One-to-one

One-to-many

Many-to-one

Many-to-many

We have seen that in each table the primary key is used to identify each row. However, in order to move from one table to another we need at least one column from each table which identifies the same entity so that we have a common value. That column or set of columns is called the "foreign key" for that table. Figure 2.7 shows that in the PATIENT table, PATNO is the primary key and also the foreign key because its values match those of the IDNO column in the VISIT table. In the VISIT table, IDNO and SEQUN are the primary keys and MDNO is the foreign key.

Figure 2.8 shows the relationship paths among the three tables. All the preplanned relationships between our tables are not just there as a path to access the information we need; they are there to help us maintain data integrity of the database. When looking at the VISIT table, we would agree that there is something wrong with storing a visit (row in the VISIT table) for a patient who does not exist in the

PATNAME	PATNO	ADDRESS	BIRTHDATE	SEX	SSNUM
DOE	0010	225 WILSHIRE BLVD	550912	M	221002222

IDNO	SEQUN	MDNO	ADDATE	DSDATE	DIAGNOSIS
0010	001	345	851112	851112	BRONCHITIS

PHYNAME	PHYNO	DEPARTMENT	HIREDATE	SALARY
STERN	345	GENERAL MEDICINE	750312	43720

Fig. 2.7 Set of related rows from different tables.

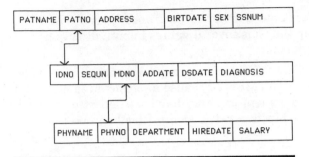

Fig. 2.8   Path among three tables.

PATIENT table or with deleting a patient (row in the PATIENT table) who has at least one row in the VISIT table. In other words, ref-
erential integrity is a very important aspect in a DB2 environment.
This is one aspect for which the database administrator (DBA) must
plan ahead to ensure the integrity of the databases by establishing the
rules for updating tables. A database is useful only if it contains con-
sistent data. We must precisely specify the operations that we want
DB2 to perform in processing data.

2.2   Structured Query Language (SQL)

SQL is the language that operates on the data in DB2 tables. It is not
just a language for retrieving data as its name says, but it can be used
to define, update, and control the tables. SQL is a very powerful language. Its statements can be used interactively as an ad hoc query
language or they can be embedded in an application program written
in Cobol, Fortran, PL/1, or Assembler. SQL is a nonprocedural language, which means we need only to specify the desired result and
DB2 will figure out the steps to get to the data. All the decisions on
what access path (i.e., indexes, etc.) to choose to get to the data or
what access paths are available are made automatically by DB2. We
will see that in a DB2 environment, the automatic database naviga-
tion and the automatic access path selection features are so useful
that they allow programmers or database designers to concentrate
more on their program logic or table design.

3

Describing Tables to DB2

We've seen that the logical data structure of a DB2 database is a set of related tables. We will talk about the physical structure of DB2 databases in Chapter 7. In this chapter we'll see how the structure of a table is defined to DB2, introduce the communication area used by DB2, and see how our application program operates in a DB2 environment.

3.1 Design Consideration

A database is usually designed for several applications and also for a variety of groups of users. Therefore, the data in the tables must be grouped in such a way that it will satisfy the users' needs for one or more applications. In a DB2 environment, although we can modify our database design very easily by adding columns to or removing columns from our tables, a modification of our design after its implementation normally entails a disruption in our applications.

3.1.1 The Caring Hospital tables and key fields

When the Caring Hospital database was designed, we had to decide not only which fields should be grouped together in one table, but also which column in each table should be the primary or foreign key column. For the purpose of this book, we are only concerned with the patients' data, their visits, and their physicians' data. Thus, our database consists of the three tables shown in Chapter 2: the PATIENT, VISIT, and PHYSICIAN tables. We also have the information each of our tables carries and how our tables are related to each other. Now, we need to implement our database design, which means we need to define our tables to DB2.

3.2 Creating the Tables

In order to define a table to DB2, we need to give each of our tables a name. Each table name consists of two parts: a prefix and a name separated by a period. The prefix is the authorization ID of the person who creates the table; we call it the "qualifier." If a table name is created without a qualifier, DB2 will automatically qualify it with the authorization ID of its creator. The name can be any alphanumeric string up to 18 characters long and must be unique within each qualifier. Each name must start with an alpha character followed by zero or more alphanumeric characters or underscores. We cannot use any of the DB2 reserved words as a name (see Appendix D for the list of these reserved words).

In our database, we have three tables with the following names: PATIENT, VISIT, and PHYSICIAN. Suppose that our authorization ID is TEST; the qualified names of our tables will be: TEST.PATIENT, TEST.VISIT, and TEST.PHYSICIAN. DB2 will not allow us to create another table with any of these names.

Now that we have decided on our table names, we need to choose the columns that make up each table. Within a table, each column must possess a unique name, but different tables can have the same column name. Each name can be any alphanumeric field up to 18 characters long and follows the same convention as the table name. The maximum number of columns we can define in a single DB2 table is 300. In our database, the PATIENT table has six columns: PATNAME, PATNO, ADDRESS, BIRTHDATE, SEX, and SSNUM. The PHYSICIAN table has five columns and the VISIT table has six. Notice that each column is named differently within each table, but we can use the same column name in different tables (we can use PATNO as the name for column IDNO in table VISIT if we wish).

Each column in a table can be considered as a field in a record; thus we have to decide the types of data the column will contain (string or numeric) and the length of the data field. DB2 supports a variety of string and numeric data types.

Before presenting the data types, let's look at the binary numbering system of computers. Our common decimal (base 10) number system has 10 digits, 0 through 9, whereas the binary (base 2) number system has only 2 digits, 0 and 1. In any computer system, data are represented in binary by a combination of bits which are digits 0 and 1. In an IBM computer with System/370 architecture, which is normally what DB2 runs on, a "byte" is the minimal addressable unit and consists of 8 bits. The System/370 uses the Extended Binary-Coded-

Decimal Interchange Code (EBCDIC) to represent characters internally in the computer. Each character is represented in a byte, or 8 bits. Thus, a byte can represent up to 256 different characters by different bit combinations of the letters A through Z, the numbers 0 through 9, and all the special characters such as @, #, $, etc. For example, the bit combination 1100 0001 represents the letter A, 1100 0010 represents the letter B, and 1111 0001 represents the number 1. However, for character sets used by national languages such as Japanese or Chinese, there are more symbols than can be represented by the 256-single-byte EBCDIC positions. Therefore, each character requires 2 bytes to represent it, and we call them the Double-Byte Character Set (DBCS).

Returning to data types, for string data type there are six types:

Data type	Meaning
CHAR(n)	Character strings contain n number of characters. We can pick any integer from 1 to 254 for n.
VARCHAR(n)	Character strings contain a variable number of characters with a maximum of n characters; n is an integer greater than 0. Normally, the value of n should be less than or equal to 254; otherwise certain restrictions apply when these columns are used in SQL statements. We will discuss these restrictions in later chapters.
LONG VARCHAR	Character strings contain a variable number of characters. The maximum number of characters is calculated by DB2.
GRAPHIC(n)	Graphic strings contain n double-byte characters; n must be from 1 to 127. Notice that because graphic strings contain double-byte characters, the maximum length is only 127, which is 254 divided by 2.
VARGRAPHIC(n)	Graphic strings contain a variable number of double-byte characters with a maximum of n characters; n is an integer greater than 0. Normally, the value of n should be less than or equal to 127; otherwise certain restrictions apply when using these columns in SQL statements. These restrictions will be explained later.
LONG VARGRAPHIC	Graphic strings contain a variable number of double-byte characters. The maximum number of characters is calculated by DB2.
DATE	Data type containing dates.
TIME	Data type containing times.

A column is called a "short string" column if it is either a fixed-length string [CHAR(n)] or a variable-length string [VARCHAR(n)] and n is less than or equal to 254. For graphic strings [GRAPHIC(n) or

VARGRAPHIC(n)], a column is called a short string column if n is less than or equal to 127. A column is called a "long string" column if it is not a short string column.

For numeric data type there are four categories:

Data type	Meaning
SMALLINT	Small integers; their value can be from $-32,768$ to $+32,767$.
INTEGER	Large integers; their value can be from $-2,147,483,648$ to $+2,147,483,647$.
FLOAT	Floating point numbers or exponential numbers; their value can be from $5.4E - 79$ to $7.2E + 75$.
DECIMAL(m,n)	Decimal numbers with m as the total number of digits and n as the number of digits in the fractional part of the number; m must be greater than 0 and less than 16 and n must be greater than or equal to 0 and less than or equal to m.

All the above limitations on the data types are based on an IBM with System/370 architecture. Readers may want to refer to manuals for their own installations to find the limitations that apply to them.

3.2.1   The PATIENT table

The primary key for the PATIENT table is the patient identification number. The table contains personal data about each patient. Figure 3.1a shows the field lengths in the PATIENT table and Figure 3.1b shows the SQL statement to create the table.

3.2.2   The PHYSICIAN table

The PHYSICIAN table contains all the information related to each physician; the primary key is the physician identification number.

PATNAME	PATNO	ADDRESS		BIRTHDATE	SEX	SSNUM	
1	10 11	14 15		44 45	50 51	52	60

(a)

```
CREATE TABLE test.patient
     ( patname        varchar(10)     not null,
       patno          char(4)         not null,
       address        varchar(30)         ,
       birthdate      char(6)             ,
       sex            char(1)         not null,
       ssnum          char(9)         not null with default )
```

(b)

Fig. 3.1 (a) PATIENT table fields lengths. (b) SQL statement to create PATIENT table.

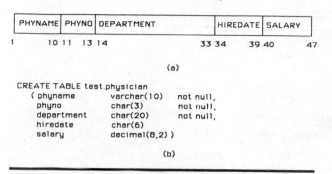

Fig. 3.2 (a) Physician table field lengths and (b) SQL statement to create PHYSICIAN table.

Figure 3.2a shows the field lengths in the PHYSICIAN table and Figure 3.2b shows how to define it to DB2.

3.2.3 The VISIT table

The VISIT table contains all the information related to each patient visit. The primary key is the patient ID and the sequence number. Figure 3.3a shows the field lengths in the VISIT table and Figure 3.3b shows how to define it to DB2.

3.3 The CREATE TABLE Statement

The keyword CREATE TABLE defines a table to DB2. We must provide the name of the table, the names of the columns, and their data types. Moreover, we can specify default values for columns that do not have meaningful values. If we do not specify anything after the data type, whenever we insert a row into the table without providing a value for that column, DB2 will give that column a special value called the "null value," meaning that no data have been supplied. When we specify NOT NULL, that means the column cannot contain a null value and we must supply a nonnull value for that column every time we insert a row into the table. NOT NULL WITH DEFAULT means that the column cannot contain a null value, but it will have a default value. If we do not provide a nonnull value for that column when we insert a row into a table, DB2 will give that column a default value depending on its data type.

Numeric data types (i.e., SMALLINT, INTEGER, FLOAT, and DECIMAL) will receive a 0 as the default value. Fixed-length string data types (i.e., CHAR and GRAPHIC) will receive blanks as default values and varying-length string data types (i.e., VARCHAR, LONG VARCHAR, VARGRAPHIC, and LONG VARGRAPHIC) will receive

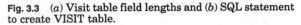

PATNO	SEQUN	MDNO	ADDATE	DSDATE	DIAGNOSIS

```
1     4 5    7 8   10 11    16 17   22 23                      42
```

(a)

```
CREATE TABLE test.visit
   ( idno          char(4)       not null,
     sequn         char(3)       not null,
     mdno          char(3)       not null,
     addate        char(6)       not null,
     dsdate        char(6)                 ,
     diagnosis     varchar(20)   not null with default )
```

(b)

Fig. 3.3   (a) Visit table field lengths and (b) SQL statement
to create VISIT table.

a string with length of 0 (or empty string) as default value. The CRE-
ATE statement can be used interactively or can be embedded in an
application program. The programming requirements will be discussed at the end of this chapter and in Chapter 4.

In the PATIENT table defined by the CREATE statement in Figure
3.1b, we decided that every time a new row is inserted into the table or
a new patient is admitted, the columns PATNAME, PATNO, and SEX
will always have a nonnull value, but the columns ADDRESS,
BIRTHDATE, and SSNUM may not have a value. However, we want
the column SSNUM to contain blanks if it does not have a value.

The person who creates a table is the table "owner." No one can access data from that table without being authorized to do so by the table owner or the database administrator (DBA). Anyone can create tables once he or she is granted the authorization by the DBA. The
statements in Figures 3.1b, 3.2b, and 3.3b are the simplest forms of
the CREATE statement. Figure 3.4 illustrates the general form of the
CREATE statement.

In Figure 3.4, all the capital letters located on the right of the ver-
tical bar are keywords; they must be coded exactly as shown. The
spaces shown between the keywords and parameters are for legibility
purpose only; DB2 requires only one space in between them. Basically,
we can divide the statement into two sections: a required section and
an optional section. In the required section, we can specify as many
columns as we want, up to 300. The columns are separated by a
comma and are enclosed in a pair of parentheses. Each column can
take one of the four forms. We've seen the first three forms in previous
examples. The fourth form is used only when a short string column
has a field procedure (routine) to encode and decode its string value.
With it, we need to provide the program name after the keyword

```
Required    CREATE TABLE table-name (
   1-          column-name  data-type,
   2-          column-name  data-type NOT NULL,
   3-          column-name  data-type NOT NULL WITH DEFAULT,
   4-          column-name  data-type FIELDPROC program-name,
               ....
               ....
               ....
               ....
               .... )

Optional    IN database-name.tablespace-name
            IN tablespace-name
            IN DATABASE database-name

            EDITPROC   program-name
            VALIDPROC  program-name
```

Fig. 3.4   General format of CREATE statement.

FIELDPROC. With FIELDPROC, we can use the key expression NOT NULL but cannot use NOT NULL WITH DEFAULT. For example, in our PHYSICIAN table, suppose we want to sort the table by the DE-PARTMENT column, but instead of sorting in alphabetical order, we want the departments to appear in a certain order of our choice; we want "General Medicine" to appear first and then "Pediatrics." We must then provide a routine to encode and decode the values of the DEPARTMENT column to obtain the correct sorting sequence. Normally, a field procedure is used to modify the sorting sequence of values in a column and it is provided when the program is installed.

3.3.1   The IN clause

The IN clause in the optional section is used to specify the database and the table space in which our table is created. In DB2, the term "table space" refers to the physical spaces used to store records of one or more tables; a database is a collection of table spaces and index spaces. We will discuss these topics in detail in Chapters 7 and 8 when we talk about the physical structure of DB2 databases and how to define them. We can use any one of the three variations of the IN clause or none. If we don't use the IN clause as in our examples in Figures 3.1b, 3.2b, and 3.3b, DB2 will use the DSNDB04 default for the database and table name and implicitly generate a table space for us. DB2 will use the table name as the name of the table space if all the following three conditions exist:

The table name has eight or fewer characters.

The table name begins with a character and contains only alphanumeric characters.

There is no other table space name or index space name in the database that has the table name.

Otherwise DB2 will give the table space an eight-character name composed of the first four characters of the table name followed by a digit and three letters that DB2 picks to make the name unique. The following are some rules that we need to observe when using the IN clause:

When specifying a database name, the database must already be defined to DB2 or must be the default database DSNDB04.

When specifying a table space name, it cannot be one that was implicitly created by DB2. The table space must already be defined and belong to DSNDB04 or to the database if one is specified.

3.3.2 The EDITPROC clause

The EDITPROC clause is similar to a field procedure except that it deals with a whole table row instead of a single column. An edit procedure, if coded, is called every time a row is updated, inserted, or retrieved.

3.3.3 The VALIDPROC clause

The VALIDPROC clause is used when we have a validation procedure to validate the value of each column every time a row is updated or inserted. A typical use of a validation routine is to validate the date entered (i.e., the month must be between 1 and 12, and the day must be between 1 and 31).

Example 3.1   The CREATE statement in Figure 3.1*b* can be coded as follows:

```
CREATE TABLE test.patient
    ( patname        varchar(10)        not null,
      patno          char(4)            not null,
      address        varchar(30)            ,
      birthdate      char(6)                ,
      sex            char(1)            not null,
      ssnum          char(9)            not null with default )
    IN DATABASE DSNDB04
```

Since a table space name is not specified, DB2 would implicitly create a table space for us and assign PATIENT as its name if there is nothing in DSNDB04 that already has that name. Suppose we have a database already defined named CARING, a table space called LEARNING that belongs to the database CARING, and a validation procedure named CHECKING. Our PATIENT table can be defined as follows:

```
CREATE TABLE test.patient
    ( patname        varchar(10)        not null,
```

```
patno           char(4)              not null,
address         varchar(30)               ,
birthdate       char(6)                   ,
sex             char(1)              not null,
ssnum           char(9)              not null with default )
IN CARING.LEARNING
VALIDPROC CHECKING
```

DB2 keeps all the information that we define to it in the DB2 catalog, which is a set of tables used by DB2 to keep track of things defined to it (i.e., table spaces, tables, databases, etc.). The data in the
catalog tables are mainly used by DB2; however, authorized DB2 users are allowed to use SQL statements to retrieve information from
the catalog tables. DB2 maintains and updates the catalog tables during
its normal operation. For each table that we created, one row would be
inserted into each of the following four tables in the DB2 catalog:

SYSIBM.SYSTABLESPACE

SYSIBM.SYSCOLUMNS

SYSIBM.SYSTABLES

SYSIBM.SYSTABAUTH

There are approximately 30 tables in the DB2 catalog. See Appendix
A for a full description of each table.

3.4   The COMMENT ON Statement

In a database environment, sometimes we want to keep some comments about a database which we can refer to in the future to help us
remember why we designed it that way. In a DB2, we can use the SQL
statement COMMENT ON to add new comments to a table or any of
its columns or to replace existing comments. There are three formats
for the COMMENT ON statement; the first format puts comments in
a table:

```
COMMENT ON TABLE table-name
    IS text-string
```

The second puts comments in one column:

```
COMMENT ON COLUMN table-name.column-name
    IS text-string
```

And the third puts comments in several columns:

```
COMMENT ON table-name:
( column-name IS text-string,
 ...          ...              ,
    column-name IS text-string )
```

The SQL COMMENT ON statement can be used interactively or can be embedded in an application program. After a COMMENT ON statement is executed, the comments are stored in the column named REMARKS of SYSIBM.SYSCOLUMNS and SYSIBM.SYSTABLES tables in the DB2 catalog with their table and columns description. Comments cannot be more than 254 characters long.

Example 3.2   This example puts comments in the PATIENT table using each of the three above formats:

```
COMMENT ON TABLE test.patient
    IS 'this table contains patients identification data'

COMMENT ON COLUMN test.patient.patname
    IS 'this column contains the patient name'

COMMENT ON test.patient
    (patno IS 'patient identification number' ,
address IS 'patient address'                 ,
ssnum IS 'patient social security number')
```

3.5   The CREATE SYNONYM Statement

We've seen that each table name consists of two parts: the authorization ID of the table owner and a name. If we are the owner of a table, when we refer to it we don't have to qualify it with our authorization ID. However. if we are using someone else's table, we must precede the table with its owner's authorization ID. The SQL CREATE SYNONYM statement allows us to create a synonym or an alternative name for an existing table so that the table can be referred to without having to use its qualified name. The CREATE SYNONYM can be embedded in an application program or used interactively; it has the following format:

```
CREATE SYNONYM synonym
    FOR table-name
```

Example 3.3   To create a synonym named JDEPT for a table called JOE.DEPT:

```
CREATE SYNONYM jdept
    FOR joe.dept
```

After the statement in Example 3.3 is executed, we can refer to the JOE.DEPT table by its synonym JDEPT. We can create a synonym for our own table or for someone else's table, but we must remember that each synonym is only valid for the person who creates it. In other words we can create a synonym JDEPT for JOE.DEPT table, but someone else can create a synonym DEPARTMENT for the same table. Each synonym is an alphanumeric string up to 18 characters and must not match any of our existing synonyms or any of our unqualified table names.

3.6 SQL Communication Area (SQLCA)

Let's take a look now at how the application program interfaces with the DB2 table to access the data in the DB2 database. The SQLCA helps our program communicate with DB2.

3.6.1 Programming requirements

Your program must have an SQLCA reserved in order to execute SQL statements. Figure 3.5 shows the coding for a Cobol program that will establish this communication area. We can see that all embedded SQL statements must start with the word EXEC SQL and end with a host language delimiter which is END-EXEC in Cobol. A semicolon (;) is used as the language delimiter if the application program is written in PL/1.

3.6.2 Program preparation

Before we can compile our program, we need to invoke the DB2 precompiler to validate and change all the embedded SQL statements into valid statements in the host language (i.e., Cobol); in most cases they are CALL statements to the DB2 language interface module. The DB2 precompiler also produces a partitioned data set, the database request module (DBRM), which contains information about each SQL statement in our program. For the SQLCA, the precompiler will generate a structure as shown in Figure 3.6.

We are now ready to compile and link-edit our program. The last step we need to take before we can execute our program is to establish a linkage between our program and DB2 tables; this is called "binding." This process creates a control structure, the application plan, for DB2 to use to access the data when the program is executed. Since DB2 keeps track of the application plan and the DBRM in the DB2 system catalog, the binding process needs to be done only once. For informa-

```
DATA DIVISION.

WORKING-STORAGE SECTION.


    EXEC SQL INCLUDE SQLCA END-EXEC.

PROCEDURE DIVISION.
```

Fig. 3.5 Sample of SQLCA coding in a Cobol program.

```
WORKING-STORAGE SECTION.

01 SQLCA.
   05 SQLCAID        PIC X(8).
   05 SQLCABC        PIC S9(9) COMP.
   05 SQLCODE        PIC S9(9) COMP.
   05 SQLERRM.
      49 SQLERRML     PIC S9(4) COMP.
      49 SQLERRMC     PIC X(70).
   05 SQLERRP        PIC X(8).
   05 SQLERRD OCCURS 6 TIMES PIC S9(9) COMP.
   05 SQLWARN.
      10 SQLWARN0     PIC X(1).
      10 SQLWARN1     PIC X(1).
      10 SQLWARN2     PIC X(1).
      10 SQLWARN3     PIC X(1).
      10 SQLWARN4     PIC X(1).
      10 SQLWARN5     PIC X(1).
      10 SQLWARN6     PIC X(1).
      10 SQLWARN7     PIC X(1).
   05 SQLEXT         PIC X(8).
```

Fig. 3.6   SQLCA structure.

tion on how to precompile, compile, link-edit, and bind our application program, please refer to the procedures available in your manuals, or the DBA at your installation should be able to provide you the necessary information on how to prepare your application program for execution. Figure 3.7 shows the program preparation process.

3.6.3 Executing a DB2 program

Figure 3.8 shows a sample Job Control Language (JCL) for an application program to be run in batch mode under the TSO Terminal Monitor Program (TMP).

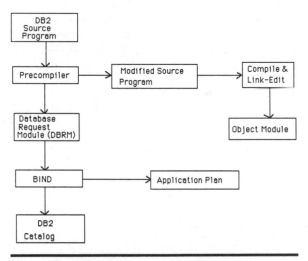

Fig. 3.7   Program preparation process.

```
//LA*TEST JOB USER=NEWDB2ID,MSGCLASS=A
//GO     EXEC PGM=IKJEFTO1,DYNAMNBR=20
//STEPLIB DD   DSN=DB2.DSNLIB,DISP=SHR
//SYSTSPRT DD   SYSOUT=*
//SYSTSPRT DD   *
DSN SYSTEM (TESTSYS)
RUN PROG  (TESTPROG)
PLAN      (TESTPLAN)
LIB       (TEST.PROGLIB)
END
/*
```

Fig. 3.8 Sample JCL for a batch program.

In any job step for a batch program, the EXEC statement invokes the TSO TMP. The STEPLIB card points to the library in which the DSN Command Processor resides. We specify the DB2 subsystem in the SYSTEM parameter, the program to be run in the PROG parameter, and the application plan in the PLAN parameter. The LIB parameter, if present, specifies the data set which contains the program to be run. Otherwise, the default data set name is "userprefix.RUNLIB.LOAD."

4

Database Retrieval

We've learned how to describe tables to DB2. In this chapter, we'll see how data can be retrieved from DB2 tables and we'll look at a DB2 batch application program. We'll use a sample listing of a program that retrieves data from the PATIENT table to point out the differences between a DB2 batch program and a regular batch program. We'll also learn how to code a DB2 batch program.

4.1 The SELECT Statement

Unlike conventional database interface languages, an SQL SELECT statement is like an English sentence in which we describe the condition(s) under which we want to retrieve the data elements. The SELECT statement can be used interactively or it can be embedded in an application program. Since there are some slight differences between an interactive SELECT statement and an embedded SELECT statement, we will discuss each statement in a separate section.

4.2 The Interactive SELECT Statement

The interactive SELECT statement is used to retrieve DB2 data; the result table is displayed at the terminal. The statement consists of several clauses or parts. The clauses must be in the following order when they are used to specify one or more conditions for retrieving DB2 data:

```
SELECT ALL | DISTINCT | table name.column name ...
   FROM table name ...
   WHERE condition ...
   GROUP BY column name ...
```

```
HAVING condition ...
ORDER BY column name | integer ASC :DESC:
```

4.2.1 The SELECT clause

The SELECT clause is used to select the columns to be produced in the result table. We can use the parameter DISTINCT to tell DB2 to keep only one single occurrence of each set of duplicate rows of the final result table. The default is ALL, which is to keep all rows of the final result table. When we want to retrieve all the existing columns in a given table, instead of having to list all the columns by name, DB2 allows us to use an asterisk (*) to indicate "all columns." It is not necessary to qualify the column names with their table name, but for documentation purpose, we normally qualify them. In the SELECT clause, we can retrieve not only existing columns in our tables, but also newly calculated columns from those existing columns. We can retrieve up to 300 columns.

4.2.2 The FROM clause

The FROM clause is used to specify one or more tables in the DB2 catalog from which the columns are extracted.

Example 4.1   To show all the rows in the PHYSICIAN table, use the following code:

```
SELECT *
    FROM TEST.PHYSICIAN
```

The result table is:

PHYNAME	PHYNO	DEPARTMENT	HIREDATE	SALARY
stern	345	general medicine	750312	43720
mitchum	867	obstetrics	661211	58760
miller	234	dermatology	670423	59670
thompson	432	neurology	760322	76540
burton	479	cardiology	470506	85786
jones	916	pediatrics	731205	49658
stein	612	general medicine	801115	43658

Example 4.2   To show every physician's ID, department, and monthly salary, use the following code:

```
SELECT physician.phyno, physician.department, physician.salary / 12
    FROM TEST.PHYSICIAN
```

The result table is:

PHYNO	DEPARTMENT	
345	general medicine	3643.333333333
867	obstetrics	4896.666666666
234	dermatology	4972.500000000
432	neurology	6378.333333333
479	cardiology	7148.833333333
916	pediatrics	4138.166666666
612	general medicine	3638.166666666

The third column in the result table in the example that is without a heading is the monthly salary of each physician. Since the third column is a newly calculated column by DB2, it does not have a heading. DB2 uses the following formulas to give the precision (precision in the total number of digits in a decimal number) and scale (scale is the total number of digits to the right of the decimal point) to the result of a decimal arithmetic operation in an SQL statement. Let p_1, s_1, p_2, and s_2 represent the precision and scale of the first and second operands, respectively. The precision p and scale s of the result is calculated as follows:

For addition and subtraction:

$$p = \text{MIN}(15, \text{ MAX}(p_1 - s_1, p_2 - s_2) + \text{MAX}(s_1, s_2) + 1)$$
$$s = \text{MAX}(s_1, s_2)$$

For multiplication:

$$p = \text{MIN}(15, p_1 + p_2)$$
$$s = \text{MAX}(15, s_1 + s_2)$$

For division:

$$p = 15$$
$$s = 15 - p_1 + s_1 - s_2$$

In Example 4.2, the precision and scale of SALARY column are 8 and 2. The precision and scale of 12 are 12 and 0. The monthly salary is calculated by dividing the annual salary by 12:

$$p_1 = 8 \qquad s_1 = 2 \qquad p_2 = 12 \qquad s_2 = 0$$
$$p = 15$$
$$s = 15 - p_1 + s_1 - s_2$$
$$\quad = 15 - 8 + 2 - 0$$
$$\quad = 9$$

Example 4.3   To show all distinct departments in the PHYSICIAN table, use the following code:

```
SELECT DISTINCT physician.department
     FROM TEST.PHYSICIAN
```

The result table is:

DEPARTMENT
general medicine
obstetrics
dermatology
neurology
cardiology
pediatrics

DB2 only displays one single occurrence of each department because the keyword DISTINCT is used.

Example 4.4   To list all departments and physician names in the PHYSICIAN table, use the following code:

```
SELECT department, phyname
     FROM TEST.PHYSICIAN
```

The result table is:

DEPARTMENT	PHYNAME
general medicine	stern
obstetrics	mitchum
dermatology	miller
neurology	thompson
cardiology	burton
pediatrics	jones
general medicine	stein

Notice that in Example 4.4, the columns in the result table appear in the order we specify them in the SELECT statement but not in their order in the PHYSICIAN table.

4.2.3   The WHERE clause

The WHERE clause is used to limit the selection to data from rows that satisfy one or more selection criteria. The number of rows we retrieve depends on the number of rows that meet the search criteria.

Example 4.5   The following selects patient ID, patient name, and sex of all the male patients in the PATIENT table:

```
SELECT patno, patname, sex
    FROM TEST.PATIENT
    WHERE sex = 'M'
```

The result table is:

PATNO	PATNAME	SEX
0001	smith	m
0010	doe	m
0003	adams	m
0020	johnson	m
0042	lee	m

Example 4.6   To select physician name, physician ID, and salary of all physicians in the PHYSICIAN table whose monthly salary is greater than $5000, use the following code:

```
SELECT phyname, phyno, salary
    FROM TEST.PHYSICIAN
    WHERE (salary / 12) > 5000
```

The result table is:

PHYNAME	PHYNO	SALARY
thompson	432	76540
burton	479	85786

Example 4.7   This code lists the names of all physicians who have a salary greater than $50,000:

```
SELECT phyname, salary
    FROM TEST.PHYSICIAN
    WHERE 50000 > salary
```

The result table is:

PHYNAME	SALARY
mitchum	58760
miller	59670
thompson	76540
burton	85786

The comparison operator in the WHERE clause can be any of the following:

=	Equal to
° =	Not equal to
<	Less than
>	Greater than
< = or ° >	Less than or equal to
> = or ° <	Greater than or equal to

The expression used in the WHERE clause can be one of three types. It can begin with a column name as in Example 4.5, it can begin with an expression with arithmetic operator(s) (+ , −, *, /) as in Example 4.6, or it can begin with a constant as in Example 4.7. Notice that character data are enclosed in single apostrophes and numeric data are not. When coding the comparison expressions, we should never try to compare numbers with strings; character strings and graphic strings are also not comparable. The expressions on both sides of the comparison operator in a WHERE clause must have the same data type. We can also use the NOT keyword to specify the opposite result of the expression. Example 4.5 can be coded using the NOT keyword as follows:

```
SELECT patno, patname, sex
    FROM TEST.PATIENT
    WHERE NOT sex = 'F'
```

DB2 also allows us to connect multiple conditions in one clause by using the logical operators AND and OR. If more than two conditions are connected by the keywords AND or OR, parentheses should be used to avoid misinterpretation.

Example 4.8   To list all physicians who were hired after 1980 and earn more than $40,000 or all physicians who make more than $70,000, use the following code:

```
SELECT *
    FROM TEST.PHYSICIAN
    WHERE (hiredate > '800000' AND salary > 40000)
          OR (salary > 70000)
```

The result table is:

PHYNAME	PHYNO	DEPARTMENT	HIREDATE	SALARY
thompson	432	neurology	760322	76540
burton	479	cardiology	470506	85786
stein	612	general medicine	801115	43658

When selecting data from each row using the WHERE clause, DB2 allows us to test that the value of a column is within a range of values by using the key expression BETWEEN x AND y. Example 4.9 shows a SELECT statement using these key expressions.

Example 4.9 To list all physicians whose salary is between $40,000 and $50,000, use the following:

```
SELECT *
    FROM TEST.PHYSICIAN
    WHERE salary BETWEEN 40000 AND 50000
```

The result table is:

PHYNAME	PHYNO	DEPARTMENT	HIREDATE	SALARY
stern	345	general medicine	750312	43720
jones	916	pediatrics	731205	49658
stein	612	general medicine	801115	43658

The key expression BETWEEN x AND y allows us to test for a value within a continuous range. But when we want to test for a number of discrete values, we can use the keyword OR. However when connecting a large number of conditions using the keyword OR, the SELECT statement can be very lengthy and hard to understand. DB2 provides us with a key expression IN (x,y,z) to use in those situations. Example 4.10 shows a SELECT statement using the keyword OR and Example 4.11 shows the same example using the key expression IN (x,y,z).

Example 4.10 To list all the patient visits with the following three physicians: 234, 612, and 345:

```
SELECT *
    FROM TEST.VISIT
    WHERE mdno = '234' OR mdno = '612' OR mdno = '345'
```

The result table is:

IDNO	SEQUN	MDNO	ADDATE	DSDATE	DIAGNOSIS
0001	001	234	850810	850810	itching
0001	002	612	851020	851020	flu
0010	001	345	851112	851112	bronchitis
0028	001	234	860520	860520	skin rash
0042	001	345	860617	860617	chest pains

Example 4.11   Using the key expression IN (x.y.z), the code is:

```
SELECT *
   FROM TEST.VISIT
   WHERE mdno IN ( '234', '612', '345' )
```

When dealing with string data, we often want to search strings that begin with, contain, or end with some common characters. DB2 allows us to use two special characters: the percent sign (%) and the underscore sign (_) to specify a wildcard of zero or more unknown characters. Those special characters are used with the keyword LIKE to specify a character string that has some particular characters we want to select. Those special characters can be in any position in a string. The underscore means "any single character" and the percent sign means "any string of zero or more characters."

Example 4.12   To list all the physicians whose name begins with the letter m, use the following:

```
SELECT *
   FROM TEST.PHYSICIAN
   WHERE phyname LIKE 'm%'
```

The result table is:

PHYNAME	PHYNO	DEPARTMENT	HIREDATE	SALARY
mitchum	867	obstetrics	661211	58760
miller	234	dermatology	670423	59670

The condition "WHERE phyname LIKE 'm%' " would include any name from one with the single character m up to a name of 10 characters beginning with a letter m, because the PHYNAME column is defined as a 10-character column.

Example 4.13   The following code lists all the physicians whose ID begins with 3 and ends with 5:

```
SELECT *
   FROM TEST.PHYSICIAN
   WHERE phyno LIKE '3_5'
```

The result table is:

PHYNAME	PHYNO	DEPARTMENT	HIREDATE	SALARY
stern	345	general medicine	750312	43720

The condition "WHERE phyno LIKE '3_5'" would include any three-character physician ID from 305 to 395 because the PHYNO column is defined as a three-character column and contains only digits.

4.2.4 Using built-in functions

Before discussing the next clause in the SELECT statement, let's look at some built-in functions that we can use in our SELECT statement to obtain some calculated values based on column values of rows that satisfy our search criteria. The five SQL built-in functions and their uses are:

COUNT (*)	Give the number of rows that satisfy the search criteria. The result is always a large integer.
COUNT (DISTINCT column name)	This is the same COUNT function as above, but when it is used with the keyword DISTINCT, it gives the number of distinct values in a particular column.
AVG (column name)	Give the average values of one or more columns. The column or columns being averaged must have a numeric data type. If the argument is integer, the result will be a large integer. If the argument is decimal, the result will be decimal with precision equal to 15 and scale equal to $15 - p_1 + s_1$, where p_1 and s_1 are the precision and scale of the argument.
MAX (column name)	Give the largest value in one or more columns. The result will have the same data type as the argument.
MIN (column name)	Give the smallest value in one or more columns. The result will have the same data type as the argument.
SUM (column name)	Give the sum of the values of one or more columns. The column or columns being summarized must have a numeric data type. If the argument is integer, the result will be a large integer. If the argument is decimal, the result will be decimal with precision equal to 15 and scale equal to the scale of the argument.

Example 4.14   This code calculates the average salary, the minimum salary, the maximum salary, the total salary, and the total number of physicians:

```
SELECT AVG (salary), MIN (salary), MAX (salary),
    SUM (salary), COUNT (*)
    FROM TEST.PHYSICIAN
```

The result table is:

AVG (salary)	MIN (salary)	MAX (salary)	SUM (salary)	COUNT (*)
59684.57	14243658.00	85786.00	417792.00	07

The calculated result columns normally do not have a heading, but for identification purposes, those columns are shown with one. DB2 does not allow the functions to be nested, which means the argument of a function must not include a function. When the keyword DISTINCT is used, DB2 will eliminate all the duplicate values.

Example 4.15   This code lists all the different departments in the PHYSICIAN table:

```
SELECT COUNT (DISTINCT department)
    FROM TEST.PHYSICIAN
```

The result table is:

COUNT (DISTINCT department)
006

4.2.5 The GROUP BY clause

The GROUP BY clause is used to divide the rows that satisfy the search criteria into groups that have common values in one or more columns. In the GROUP BY clause, we must specify one or more columns to be used for grouping the rows. GROUP BY only generates a set of groups of rows and does not sort at all. The column or columns we specify in the GROUP BY clause cannot be a long string column (refer to Chapter 3 for a definition of long string column). If more than one column is used in the GROUP BY clause, the columns must be separated by a comma.

Example 4.16:   This code displays a list of physician IDs and, for each physician ID, lists the number of patient visits:

```
SELECT mdno, COUNT(*)
    FROM TEST.VISIT
    GROUP BY mdno
```

The result table is:

MDNO	COUNT (*)
234	2
612	1
345	2
867	1
432	1
479	1
916	1

4.2.6 The HAVING clause

The HAVING clause is used to specify one or more selection criteria that each group in a GROUP BY clause must satisfy. The HAVING clause is used in conjunction with the GROUP BY clause to allow us to specify the search condition for each group rather than for individual rows in the group. The search condition specified in the HAVING clause can be any existing column(s) or function. If more than one condition is specified in the HAVING clause, the AND and OR logical operators must be used to connect them together.

Example 4.17   This code lists each physician ID and the number of visits to each physician if there is more than one visit:

```
SELECT mdno, COUNT(*)
    FROM TEST.VISIT
    GROUP BY mdno
    HAVING COUNT(*) > 1 OR mdno > '900'
```

The result table is:

MDNO	COUNT (*)
234	2
345	2
916	1

Let's compare Example 4.17 with Example 4.16. By adding the HAVING clause, we have eliminated four groups.

4.2.7 The ORDER BY clause

The ORDER BY clause is used to specify the order in which the rows in the result table are displayed. We can order the rows in ascending order by using the keyword ASC or in descending order by using the keyword DESC. If we do not specify any keyword, the default is ASC, or ascending. When using the ORDER BY clause, we must specify one or more columns in the result table we want DB2 to use to order the rows. DB2 also allows us to use an integer to identify a column in the result table; the integer must correspond to the order in which that column appears in the result table. If a column in the result table comes from an existing column, we can either use its column name or an integer to identify it. But if a column in the result table is derived from an arithmetic expression or function, we must use an integer to identify it in the ORDER BY clause. The column or columns we specify in the ORDER BY clause cannot be long string columns. If more than one column is used in the ORDER BY clause, they must be separated by a comma.

Example 4.18   This code displays physician and patient visits in the order of physician IDs:

```
SELECT mdno, COUNT (*)
    FROM TEST.VISIT
    GROUP BY mdno
    ORDER BY mdno ASC
```

The result table is:

MDNO	COUNT (*)
234	2
345	2
432	1
479	1
612	1
867	1
916	1

The rows in the result table are in ascending order by physician ID.

Example 4.19   Display physician and patient visits in the order of the number of visits and physician IDs:

```
SELECT mdno, COUNT (*)
    FROM TEST.VISIT
    GROUP BY mdno
    ORDER BY 2, mdno
```

The result table is:

MDNO	COUNT (*)
432	1
479	1
612	1
867	1
916	1
234	2
345	2

Since the COUNT (*) column is derived from a function, we have to use an integer to identify it. For the secondary sort sequence, we can either use MDNO or the integer 1 to identify it.

4.3 The Embedded SELECT Statement

The embedded SELECT statement is used to retrieve DB2 data and generate a result table consisting of only one row. The values in the result table are then assigned to an application program data area. The embedded SELECT statement can be coded exactly as an interactive SELECT statement with some minor exceptions:

We must use an additional clause, the INTO clause, to allow DB2 to put the retrieved data into our program variable or structure.

We cannot use the following clauses in the embedded SELECT statement: GROUP BY, HAVING, and ORDER BY.

The clauses in the embedded SELECT statement must be coded in the following order:

```
SELECT ALL :DISTINCT: table name.column name ...
    INTO    variable   ...
    FROM    table name ...
    WHERE   condition  ...
```

The syntax for the FROM and WHERE clauses for an embedded SELECT statement is exactly the same as for an interactive SELECT statement. The INTO clause is used to name a variable or a structure in our application program into which the values of the result row are mapped. When using an embedded SELECT statement, we must make sure that our SELECT statement returns only one row of data.

If the SELECT statement finds more than one row, it is an error and no data will be returned.

4.3.1 The retrieval program

Figure 4.1 is a complete Cobol listing of the database retrieval program. Look at the program carefully; we'll discuss it in the next section. For those of you who are familiar with PL/1 language, you can find the same program listing in PL/1 in Appendix B. In DB2, a programming language is called a "host language" if we can embed SQL statements in it (i.e., Cobol, PL/1, Fortran, etc.).

4.3.2 The working-storage section

The SQLCA coding requirement discussed in Chapter 3 is shown on line 130 in the working-storage section. Our sample program is written to access data from the PATIENT table. DB2 does not require us to describe the table(s) our program accesses, but it is a good programming practice to always describe the table(s) in our program because we can always refer to the column names and data types of the table(s) we are working with. This practice keeps our program well documented, and, also, the DB2 precompiler will use this declaration to make sure that the column names and data types we refer to are valid.

There are two ways to declare table(s) in our program. We can code a DECLARE TABLE statement as in our sample program on lines 121–128, or we can use the Declarations Generator (DCLGEN). DCLGEN is a utility supplied with DB2 which we can use to generate a DECLARE TABLE statement in a host language (Cobol or PL/1) and place it in the library we specify. Since DCLGEN uses information from the DB2 catalog, the table(s) we want to declare must already exist. The readers should refer to their installation manuals for information on how to use DCLGEN.

Lines 54–64 show a declaration of a structure in the host language used to store the column values from selected rows. In Cobol or PL/1, a structure can have many levels, but when it is defined to be used for an SQL statement, it can have at most two levels. However, in Cobol there is an exception when a varying-length variable is used which requires another level, which must be level 49. We can declare the host variables separately or combine them under one structure. Refer to Appendix C for the allowable data types of the host languages.

When using DCLGEN for table declarations, it also generates a matching host structure corresponding to the columns of a table's row. Suppose we have used DCLGEN to produce our table declaration and our record description and we've named it DCLPAT; we would replace lines 54–64 and 121–128 in our program with the following lines:

```
000010    ID DIVISION.
000020    PROGRAM-ID.  SAMPLE1.
000030    AUTHOR.  VIET G. TRAN.
000040    DATE-COMPILED.
000050    REMARKS.  THIS PROGRAM READS AN INPUT FILE CONTAINING PATIENT
000060              IDENTIFICATION NUMBERS AND PRINTS OUT THE PATIENT
000070              NAME, ADDRESS, AND SOCIAL SECURITY NUMBER.
000080
000090    ENVIRONMENT DIVISION.
000100
000110    CONFIGURATION SECTION.
000120    SOURCE-COMPUTER.  IBM-3090.
000130    OBJECT-COMPUTER.  IBM-3090.
000140    SPECIAL-NAMES.  C01 IS NEW-PAGE.
000150    INPUT-OUTPUT SECTION.
000160    FILE-CONTROL.
000170
000180        SELECT IDFILE
000190            ASSIGN TO UT-S-IDFILE.
000200
000210        SELECT OUTFILE
000220            ASSIGN TO UT-S-OUTFILE.
000230
000240    DATA DIVISION.
000250
000260    FILE SECTION.
000270
000280    FD  IDFILE
000290        LABEL RECORDS ARE STANDARD
000300        BLOCK CONTAINS 0 RECORDS
000310        RECORDING MODE IS F
000320        RECORD CONTAINS 80 CHARACTERS
000330        DATA RECORD IS ID-REC.
000340
000350    01  ID-REC                     PIC X(80).
000360
000370    FD  OUTFILE
000380        LABEL RECORDS ARE OMITTED
000390        BLOCK CONTAINS 0 RECORDS
000400        RECORDING MODE IS F
000410        RECORD CONTAINS 133 CHARACTERS
000420        DATA RECORD IS OUT-REC.
000430
000440    01  OUT-REC.
000450        05  OUT-CCTL              PIC X.
000460        05  OUT-PRT               PIC X(132).
000470
000480    WORKING-STORAGE SECTION.
000490
000500    01  WS-ID-REC.
000510        05  IDNUM                 PIC X(4).
000520        05  FILLER                PIC X(76).
000530
000540    01  PATINFO.
000550        05  NAME.
000560            49  NAMEL             PIC S9(4) COMP.
000570            49  NAMED             PIC X(10) VALUE SPACES.
000580        05  ID                    PIC X(4).
000590        05  ADDRESS.
000600            49  ADDRESSL          PIC S9(4) COMP.
```

Fig. 4.1 PATIENT table retrieval program.

```
000610              49  ADDRESSD            PIC X(30) VALUE SPACES.
000620         05  BIRTHDATE               PIC X(6).
000630         05  SEX                     PIC X(1).
000640         05  SOCSEC                  PIC X(9).
000650
000660  01  WORK-FIELDS.
000670         05  SOCNUM                  PIC X(9).
000680         05  SOCNO REDEFINES SOCNUM.
000690              10  SOCNO1             PIC X(3).
000700              10  SOCNO2             PIC X(2).
000710              10  SOCNO3             PIC X(4).
000720
000730  01  STATUS-SWITCHES.
000740         05  EOF-SWITCH              PIC X VALUE '0'.
000750              88  EOF                VALUE '1'.
000760  01  INTERNAL-COUNTS.
000770         05  LYNES                   PIC 9(2) COMP-3 VALUE 99.
000780
000790  01  HDR1.
000800         05  FILLER                  PIC X(12) VALUE
000810              'PATIENT NAME'.
000820         05  FILLER                  PIC X(05) VALUE SPACES.
000830         05  FILLER                  PIC X(10) VALUE
000840              'PATIENT ID'.
000850         05  FILLER                  PIC X(05) VALUE SPACES.
000860         05  FILLER                  PIC X(30) VALUE
000870               'ADDRESS                      '.
000880         05  FILLER                  PIC X(05) VALUE SPACES.
000890         05  FILLER                  PIC X(22) VALUE
000900              'SOCIAL SECURITY NUMBER'.
000910         05  FILLER                  PIC X(43) VALUE SPACES.
000920
000930  01  HDR2.
000940         05  FILLER                  PIC X(12) VALUE
000950              '------------'.
000960         05  FILLER                  PIC X(05) VALUE SPACES.
000970         05  FILLER                  PIC X(10) VALUE
000980              '----------'.
000990         05  FILLER                  PIC X(05) VALUE SPACES.
001000         05  FILLER                  PIC X(30) VALUE
001010              '------------------------------'.
001020         05  FILLER                  PIC X(05) VALUE SPACES.
001030         05  FILLER                  PIC X(22) VALUE
001040              '----------------------'.
001050         05  FILLER                  PIC X(43) VALUE SPACES.
001060
001070  01  DETAIL.
001080         05  RP-NAME                 PIC X(10).
001090         05  FILLER                  PIC X(7)  VALUE SPACES.
001100         05  RP-ID                   PIC X(4).
001110         05  FILLER                  PIC X(11) VALUE SPACES.
001120         05  RP-ADDRESS              PIC X(30).
001130         05  FILLER                  PIC X(5)  VALUE SPACES.
001140         05  RP-SOC-SEC1             PIC X(3).
001150         05  FILLER                  PIC X     VALUE '-'.
001160         05  RP-SOC-SEC2             PIC X(2).
001170         05  FILLER                  PIC X     VALUE '-'.
001180         05  RP-SOC-SEC3             PIC X(4).
001190         05  FILLER                  PIC X(54) VALUE SPACES.
001200
```

Fig. 4.1 *(Continued)*

```
001210          EXEC SQL DECLARE PATIENT TABLE
001220                    (PATNAME          VARCHAR(10)  NOT NULL,
001230                     PATNO            CHAR(4)      NOT NULL,
001240                     ADDRESS          VARCHAR(30),
001250                     BIRTHDATE        CHAR(6),
001260                     SEX              CHAR(1),
001270                     SSNUM            CHAR(9)      NOT NULL WITH DEFAULT)
001280              END-EXEC.
001290
001300          EXEC SQL INCLUDE SQLCA END-EXEC.
001310
001320          EJECT
001330      PROCEDURE DIVISION.
001340
001350          PERFORM 0000-INITIALIZE.
001360
001370          READ IDFILE INTO WS-ID-REC
001380                       AT END MOVE '1' TO EOF-SWITCH.
001390          PERFORM 1000-PROCESS-INPUT UNTIL EOF.
001400          PERFORM 3000-TERMINATE.
001410
001420          GOBACK.
001430
001440      0000-INITIALIZE.
001450      *--------------
001460
001470          OPEN INPUT   IDFILE
001480               OUTPUT  OUTFILE.
001490
001500          MOVE '0'   TO EOF-SWITCH.
001510          MOVE SPACES TO OUT-PRT.
001520          PERFORM 2500-HEADING-PRINT.
001530
001540      1000-PROCESS-INPUT.
001550      *-------------------
001560
001570          EXEC SQL SELECT *
001580                   INTO :PATINFO
001590                   FROM PATIENT
001600                   WHERE PATNO = :IDNUM
001610              END-EXEC.
001620
001630          IF SQLCODE EQUAL TO ZERO
001640              PERFORM 2000-LOGICAL-PRINT.
001650
001660          READ IDFILE INTO WS-ID-REC
001670                       AT END MOVE '1' TO EOF-SWITCH.
001680
001690      2000-LOGICAL-PRINT.
001700      *------------------
001710
001720          MOVE SOCSEC    TO SOCNUM.
001730          MOVE NAMED     TO RP-NAME.
001740          MOVE ID        TO RP-ID.
001750          MOVE ADDRESSD  TO RP-ADDRESS.
001760          MOVE SOCNO1    TO RP-SOC-SEC1.
001770          MOVE SOCNO2    TO RP-SOC-SEC2.
001780          MOVE SOCNO3    TO RP-SOC-SEC3.
001790
001800          IF LYNES IS GREATER THAN 57
```

Fig. 4.1 *(Continued)*

```
001810          MOVE 0 TO LYNES
001820          PERFORM 2500-HEADING-PRINT
001830      ELSE
001840          ADD 1 TO LYNES.
001850      MOVE DETAIL      TO OUT-PRT.
001860      WRITE OUT-REC AFTER ADVANCING 1.
001870
001880      MOVE SPACES      TO NAMED.
001890      MOVE SPACES      TO ADDRESSD.
001900
001910  2500-HEADING-PRINT.
001920  *------------------
001930
001940      MOVE HDR1        TO OUT-PRT.
001950      WRITE OUT-REC AFTER ADVANCING NEW-PAGE.
001960      MOVE HDR2        TO OUT-PRT.
001970      WRITE OUT-REC AFTER ADVANCING 1.
001980      MOVE 2 TO LYNES.
001990
002000  3000-TERMINATE.
002010  *--------------
002020
002030      CLOSE IDFILE
002040            OUTFILE.
```

Fig. 4.1 *(Continued)*

```
EXEC SQL
    INCLUDE dclpat
    END-EXEC
```

When we precompile our program, the DB2 precompiler will insert the table declaration and record description generated by DCLGEN into our source program. The use of DCLGEN to produce table declarations and record descriptions is preferable to the hard-coded method because if we modify the structure of our PATIENT table, we just need to invoke DCLGEN again to produce the new table declaration and record description and re-precompile all programs that use that table. The rest of the working-storage section is fairly straightforward; therefore, let's go to the next section of the program.

4.3.3 The procedure division

The program reads an input record and stores the patient identification number in a working-storage area to be used by the SELECT statement. When the SELECT statement on lines 157–161 is executed, DB2 retrieves the first row of data and stores it in the host structure PATINFO. After the SELECT statement, the program checks a field in the SQLCA to see if the retrieval was successful. If it was, the program prints one line of the report and loops back to read another input record. The rest of the program is fairly similar to any regular batch program.

Now let's look at some requirements for coding SQL statements in an application program:

Embedded SQL statements must start with the key expression EXEC SQL and end with a delimiter. EXEC and SQL must be on the same line.

Host variables are preceded with a colon; they can be used only to represent a value or column name, not a table name.

SQL, DSN, and any of the DB2 reserved words should not be used as a name for a host variable. The list of DB2 reserved words is shown in Appendix D.

As we've seen in Chapter 3, the DB2 precompiler will generate a structure for the SQLCA in the working-storage section as follows:

```
WORKING-STORAGE SECTION.
        .
        .
01 SQLCA.
     05 SQLCAID        PIC X(8).
     05 SQLCABC        PIC S9(9) COMP.
     05 SQLCODE        PIC S9(9) COMP.
     05 SQLERRM.
        49 SQLERRML    PIC S9(4) COMP.
        49 SQLERRMC    PIC X(70).
     05 SQLERRP        PIC X(8).
     05 SQLERRD OCCURS 6 TIMES PIC S9(9) COMP.
     05 SQLWARN.
        10 SQLWARN0    PIC X(1).
        10 SQLWARN1    PIC X(1).
        10 SQLWARN2    PIC X(1).
        10 SQLWARN3    PIC X(1).
        10 SQLWARN4    PIC X(1).
        10 SQLWARN5    PIC X(1).
        10 SQLWARN6    PIC X(1).
        10 SQLWARN7    PIC X(1).
     05 SQLEXT         PIC X(8).
```

The SQLCA allows DB2 to communicate with our application program. Every time an SQL statement is executed in our program, DB2 puts a value in the SQLCODE field of the SQLCA to tell the status of the statement's execution. SQLCODE is not the only field in the SQLCA that contains useful information; DB2 puts a lot of valuable information in the SQLCA structure. The following is the list of fields in the SQLCA and their meanings:

Field	Meaning
SQLCAID	An eight-character string with a value of SQLCA.
SQLCABC	A large integer with a value of 136, which indicates the length of the SQLCA.
SQLCODE	A large integer that contains a return code of the most recent SQL statement execution. Zero means a successful execution. A negative number means an error condition, and a positive number means a successful execution which con-

tains an exception condition. For example, a +100 return code means NOT FOUND or END OF FILE.

SQLERRML	A small integer with a value between 0 and 70 which specifies the length of SQLERRMC.
SQLERRMC	A varying-length string that contains actual names of fields or objects in error.
SQLERRP	An eight-character string that contains diagnostic information.
SQLERRD	An array of six large integers that contain diagnostic information. The third element, or SQLERRD(3), contains the number of rows inserted, updated, or deleted after each INSERT, UPDATE, or DELETE statement.
SQLWARN0	A warning flag that can be either W or blank. A blank value means that other warning flags are also blank. A W value means that there is at least one other warning flag that has a value of W.
SQLWARN1	A W means that a column value was truncated when assigning it to a host variable.
SQLWARN2	A W means that not null values were not used in the argument of a function.
SQLWARN3	A W means that the number of columns do not match the number of host variables.
SQLWARN4	A W means that a dynamic UPDATE or DELETE SQL statement does not have a WHERE clause. Dynamic SQL will be covered in Chapter 9.
SQLWARN5	A W value means that the SQL statement is only valid in SQL/DS but not in DB2.
SQLWARN6	Reserved for future use.
SQLWARN7	Reserved for future use.
SQLWARN8	Reserved for future use.

4.4 Retrieving Multiple Rows

After analyzing the sample program in Figure 4.1, we see that DB2 does not allow us to retrieve more than one row at a time in an embedded SELECT statement. However, one of the nice features of DB2 is the ability to retrieve and process one or more rows at a time that satisfy the search criteria. To support the multiple retrieval feature in an application program, DB2 provides a feature called a "cursor." Suppose we want to retrieve information about each patient visit and we know that each patient can have more than one visit. Figure 4.2 shows a sample program that uses a cursor to retrieve data from the VISIT table. Notice that we introduce four new SQL statements in this sample program. Basically, when we use a cursor in our application program, DB2 dynamically acquires some storage to build a tempo-

```
000010   ID DIVISION.
000020   PROGRAM-ID.   SAMPLE1.
000030   AUTHOR.   VIET G. TRAN.
000040   DATE-COMPILED.
000050   REMARKS.   THIS PROGRAM READS AN INPUT FILE CONTAINING PATIENT
000060            IDENTIFICATION NUMBERS AND PRINTS OUT THE PATIENT
000070            NAME, ADDRESS, AND SOCIAL SECURITY NUMBER.
000080
000090   ENVIRONMENT DIVISION.
000100
000110   CONFIGURATION SECTION.
000120   SOURCE-COMPUTER.   IBM-3090.
000130   OBJECT-COMPUTER.   IBM-3090.
000140   SPECIAL-NAMES.   C01 IS NEW-PAGE.
000150   INPUT-OUTPUT SECTION.
000160   FILE-CONTROL.
000170
000180       SELECT IDFILE
000190            ASSIGN TO UT-S-IDFILE.
000200
000210       SELECT OUTFILE
000220            ASSIGN TO UT-S-OUTFILE.
000230
000240   DATA DIVISION.
000250
000260   FILE SECTION.
000270
000280   FD   IDFILE
000290        LABEL RECORDS ARE STANDARD
000300        BLOCK CONTAINS 0 RECORDS
000310        RECORDING MODE IS F
000320        RECORD CONTAINS 80 CHARACTERS
000330        DATA RECORD IS ID-REC.
000340
000350   01   ID-REC                  PIC X(80).
000360
000370   FD   OUTFILE
000380        LABEL RECORDS ARE OMITTED
000390        BLOCK CONTAINS 0 RECORDS
000400        RECORDING MODE IS F
000410        RECORD CONTAINS 133 CHARACTERS
000420        DATA RECORD IS OUT-REC.
000430
000440   01   OUT-REC.
000450        05   OUT-CCTL           PIC X.
000460        05   OUT-PRT            PIC X(132).
000470
000480   WORKING-STORAGE SECTION.
000490
000500   01   WS-ID-REC.
000510        05   IDNUM              PIC X(4).
000520        05   FILLER             PIC X(76).
000530
000540   01   PATINFO.
000550        05   NAME.
000560            49   NAMEL          PIC S9(4) COMP.
000570            49   NAMED          PIC X(10) VALUE SPACES.
000580        05   ID                 PIC X(4).
000590        05   ADDRESS.
000600            49   ADDRESSL       PIC S9(4) COMP.
```

Fig. 4.2 VISIT table retrieval program.

```
000610                 49  ADDRESSD              PIC X(30) VALUE SPACES.
000620        05  BIRTHDATE                      PIC X(6).
000630        05  SEX                            PIC X(1).
000640        05  SOCSEC                         PIC X(9).
000650
000660  01  WORK-FIELDS.
000670        05  SOCNUM                         PIC X(9).
000680        05  SOCNO REDEFINES SOCNUM.
000690                 10  SOCNO1                 PIC X(3).
000700                 10  SOCNO2                 PIC X(2).
000710                 10  SOCNO3                 PIC X(4).
000720
000730  01  STATUS-SWITCHES.
000740        05  EOF-SWITCH                     PIC X VALUE '0'.
000750             88  EOF                       VALUE '1'.
000760  01  INTERNAL-COUNTS.
000770        05  LYNES                          PIC 9(2) COMP-3 VALUE 99.
000780
000790  01  HDR1.
000800        05  FILLER                         PIC X(12) VALUE
000810             'PATIENT NAME'.
000820        05  FILLER                         PIC X(05) VALUE SPACES.
000830        05  FILLER                         PIC X(10) VALUE
000840               'PATIENT ID'.
000850        05  FILLER                         PIC X(05) VALUE SPACES.
000860        05  FILLER                         PIC X(30) VALUE
000870             'ADDRESS                    '.
000880        05  FILLER                         PIC X(05) VALUE SPACES.
000890        05  FILLER                         PIC X(22) VALUE
000900             'SOCIAL SECURITY NUMBER'.
000910        05  FILLER                         PIC X(43) VALUE SPACES.
000920
000930  01  HDR2.
000940        05  FILLER                         PIC X(12) VALUE
000950             '------------'.
000960        05  FILLER                         PIC X(05) VALUE SPACES.
000970        05  FILLER                         PIC X(10) VALUE
000980             '----------'.
000990        05  FILLER                         PIC X(05) VALUE SPACES.
001000        05  FILLER                         PIC X(30) VALUE
001010             '------------------------------'.
001020        05  FILLER                         PIC X(05) VALUE SPACES.
001030        05  FILLER                         PIC X(22) VALUE
001040             '----------------------'.
001050        05  FILLER                         PIC X(43) VALUE SPACES.
001060
001070  01  DETAIL.
001080        05  RP-NAME                        PIC X(10).
001090        05  FILLER                         PIC X(7)  VALUE SPACES.
001100        05  RP-ID                          PIC X(4).
001110        05  FILLER                         PIC X(11) VALUE SPACES.
001120        05  RP-ADDRESS                     PIC X(30).
001130        05  FILLER                         PIC X(5)  VALUE SPACES.
001140        05  RP-SOC-SEC1                    PIC X(3).
001150        05  FILLER                         PIC X     VALUE '-'.
001160        05  RP-SOC-SEC2                    PIC X(2).
001170        05  FILLER                         PIC X     VALUE '-'.
001180        05  RP-SOC-SEC3                    PIC X(4).
001190        05  FILLER                         PIC X(54) VALUE SPACES.
001200
```

Fig. 4.2 *(Continued)*

```
001210          EXEC SQL DECLARE PATIENT TABLE
001220                (PATNAME          VARCHAR(10)   NOT NULL,
001230                 PATNO            CHAR(4)       NOT NULL,
001240                 ADDRESS          VARCHAR(30),
001250                 BIRTHDATE        CHAR(6),
001260                 SEX              CHAR(1),
001270                 SSNUM            CHAR(9)       NOT NULL WITH DEFAULT)
001280             END-EXEC.
001290
001300          EXEC SQL INCLUDE SQLCA END-EXEC.
001310
001320          EJECT
001330     PROCEDURE DIVISION.
001340
001350          PERFORM 0000-INITIALIZE.
001360
001370          READ IDFILE INTO WS-ID-REC
001380                   AT END MOVE '1' TO EOF-SWITCH.
001390          PERFORM 1000-PROCESS-INPUT UNTIL EOF.
001400          PERFORM 3000-TERMINATE.
001410
001420          GOBACK.
001430
001440     0000-INITIALIZE.
001450     *--------------
001460
001470          OPEN INPUT  IDFILE
001480               OUTPUT OUTFILE.
001490
001500          MOVE '0'    TO EOF-SWITCH.
001510          MOVE SPACES TO OUT-PRT.
001520          PERFORM 2500-HEADING-PRINT.
001530
001540     1000-PROCESS-INPUT.
001550     *------------------
001560
001570          EXEC SQL SELECT *
001580                 INTO :PATINFO
001590                 FROM PATIENT
001600                 WHERE PATNO = :IDNUM
001610             END-EXEC.
001620
001630          IF SQLCODE EQUAL TO ZERO
001640              PERFORM 2000-LOGICAL-PRINT.
001650
001660          READ IDFILE INTO WS-ID-REC
001670                   AT END MOVE '1' TO EOF-SWITCH.
001680
001690     2000-LOGICAL-PRINT.
001700     *------------------
001710
001720          MOVE SOCSEC     TO SOCNUM.
001730          MOVE NAMED      TO RP-NAME.
001740          MOVE ID         TO RP-ID.
001750          MOVE ADDRESSD   TO RP-ADDRESS.
001760          MOVE SOCNO1     TO RP-SOC-SEC1.
001770          MOVE SOCNO2     TO RP-SOC-SEC2.
001780          MOVE SOCNO3     TO RP-SOC-SEC3.
001790
001800          IF LYNES IS GREATER THAN 57
```

Fig. 4.2 *(Continued)*

```
001810          MOVE 0 TO LYNES
001820          PERFORM 2500-HEADING-PRINT
001830       ELSE
001840          ADD 1 TO LYNES.
001850       MOVE DETAIL      TO OUT-PRT.
001860       WRITE OUT-REC AFTER ADVANCING 1.
001870
001880       MOVE SPACES      TO NAMED.
001890       MOVE SPACES      TO ADDRESSD.
001900
001910   2500-HEADING-PRINT.
001920   *------------------
001930
001940       MOVE HDR1        TO OUT-PRT.
001950       WRITE OUT-REC AFTER ADVANCING NEW-PAGE.
001960       MOVE HDR2        TO OUT-PRT.
001970       WRITE OUT-REC AFTER ADVANCING 1.
001980       MOVE 2 TO LYNES.
001990
002000   3000-TERMINATE.
002010   *--------------
002020
002030       CLOSE IDFILE
002040             OUTFILE.
```

Fig. 4.2   *(Continued)*

rary table to hold each set of rows that satisfy the search criteria. The rows in the temporary table are then made available to the application program one at a time. The temporary table is released when a CLOSE statement is encountered.

4.4.1   The DECLARE CURSOR statement

The SQL DECLARE CURSOR statement is used to define a cursor. A cursor allows an application program to retrieve a set of rows; each row in the set is passed to the application program one at a time. A cursor also serves as a row pointer which points to the current row of the result table. The DECLARE CURSOR statement must be embedded in an application program and have the following format:

```
EXEC SQL DECLARE cursor-name CURSOR FOR
       SELECT statement ...
     language-delimiter
```

When declaring a cursor, we must give it a name and each cursor must possess a unique name within an application program. The SELECT statement embedded in the DECLARE CURSOR statement is used to specify the set of rows to be retrieved. It has the same syntax as the interactive SELECT statement and cannot contain an INTO clause.

When the statement on lines 135–139 in Figure 4.2 is executed, DB2 defines a cursor named PVISIT and selects all the rows in the VISIT table that have an ID number equal to the value of a host variable IDNUM. However, the selected rows are not available to the application program until an OPEN statement is executed.

4.4.2 The OPEN and CLOSE statements

The SQL OPEN statement is used to open a cursor. It allows DB2 to make the rows in the result table available to the application program one at a time. When a cursor is opened, it is pointed to the beginning of the result table. The SQL CLOSE statement is used to close a cursor and make the result table no longer available to the application program. DB2 will automatically close an open cursor if the application program ends without a CLOSE statement, but that will have some affect on the system performance. The OPEN and CLOSE statements must be embedded in an application program and have the following formats:

```
EXEC SQL OPEN     cursor-name
     language-delimiter

EXEC SQL CLOSE     cursor-name
     language-delimiter
```

The statement on line 167 in Figure 4.2 opens the cursor named PVISIT and the statement on line 175 closes it.

4.4.3 The FETCH statement

The SQL FETCH statement is used to move the cursor to point to the next row in the result table and retrieve the values of the row and put them into the structure or into the variables specified in the INTO clause. When a cursor is first opened, the cursor is positioned before the first row in the result table. When a FETCH statement is executed and the cursor is pointed to the last row in the result table, the cursor position will be after the last row. The FETCH statement must be embedded in an application program and have the following format:

```
EXEC SQL FETCH     cursor-name
          INTO host-structure or host-variable ...
     language-delimiter
```

If host variables are specified in the INTO clause of a FETCH statement, they must be separated by a comma. The statement on line 169 in Figure 4.2 moves the cursor to the next row and assigns its column values to the host structure VISITINFO.

Before going to the next chapter, let's look at the SQLCODE codes that can be returned as result of a SELECT statement. There are two return codes that are quite common when we're using SELECT statements; they are shown below. 000 means that our SQL statement has executed successfully. The +100 is returned if DB2 cannot find any rows that meet our selection to return.

SQLCODE

return code	Meaning
000	SUCCESSFUL EXECUTION
+ 100	ROW NOT FOUND

5

Inserting and Loading

This chapter begins an extended discussion of the database maintenance features of DB2. We've learned in earlier chapters how to define tables to DB2 and how to retrieve data from DB2 tables. In this chapter, we shall see how to insert rows into existing tables and how DB2 tables are loaded. We shall follow the pattern of previous chapters by showing the general formats and examples of each statement.

5.1 Inserting Rows into Tables

The term "inserting" refers to the process of adding one or more rows to an existing table. For example, in our Caring Hospital environment, every time a new patient is admitted to the hospital we need to add a new row or patient record to our PATIENT table, if he or she is a new patient, and add a new row to our VISIT table. Adding a new row to a DB2 table can be done by using the INSERT statement.

5.2 The INSERT statement

The SQL INSERT statement is used to add one or more rows to a DB2 table. The statement can be used interactively or it can be embedded in an application program. The only difference is that when the statement is embedded in an application program, it must start with the key expression EXEC SQL and end with a host language delimiter. The following is the general format of the INSERT statement:

```
INSERT INTO table name
       ( column-name ... )
     VALUES ( constant | host-variable | NULL | USER ... )
```

5.2.1 The INTO clause

The INTO clause is used to specify the name of the table into which we want to insert rows and the columns for which we have the values for insertion. The table specified must already be defined in the DB2 catalog and must not be any of the DB2 catalog tables. In other words, we cannot insert new rows into a nonexistent table or into DB2 catalog tables. Each column listed must belong to the table specified and cannot be listed more than once. The columns listed do not have to be in the order they are in in the table, but they must be separated by commas and enclosed in parentheses. If no column name is listed, DB2 assumes that we use all the columns.

5.2.2 The VALUES clause

The VALUES clause lists the values of the row to be inserted. The values listed can be a constant or, if the statement is embedded in an application program, the values listed can also be a host variable or a host structure. The number of column names listed in an INTO clause, if any, must be equal to the number of values listed in a VALUES clause. When the INSERT statement is executed, DB2 assigns the values in the VALUES clause to the columns in the INTO clause in the order in which they appear on the list.

Example 5.1   Suppose we wanted to insert the following row into the PATIENT table:

PATNAME	PATNO	ADDRESS	BIRTHDATE	SEX	SSNUM
burton	0002	200 century boulevard	800520	m	586529443

The following statements show how to insert the above row:

```
INSERT INTO PATIENT
    VALUES ('burton', '0002', '200 century boulevard',
        '800520', 'm', '586529443')
or
INSERT INTO PATIENT
    (patname, patno, address, birthdate, sex, ssnum)
    VALUES ('burton', '0002', '200 century boulevard',
        '800520', 'm', '586529443')
or
INSERT INTO PATIENT
    (birthdate, sex, ssnum, patname, patno, address)
    VALUES ('800520', 'm', '586529443',
        'burton', '0002', '200 century boulevard')
```

It is always advisable to list the column names in the INSERT statement because then we or someone else can always go back to look at our code and understand into which columns we're trying to insert the values. As mentioned in Chapter 3, we must at least supply the values for the columns defined as NOT NULL. Otherwise, an error will occur and no row will be inserted.

Example 5.2   Suppose at the time we add the patient record into the PATIENT table, we do not have the patient address, birthdate, or social security number. We can code the statement as follows:

```
INSERT INTO PATIENT
    (patname, patno, sex)
    VALUES ('burton', '0002', 'm')
```

After the above statement is executed, DB2 will assign a null value to the ADDRESS and BIRTHDATE fields and a blank to the social security number (SSNUM) field. We can use the keyword NULL to specify a null value and the keyword USER to specify the authorization ID in the VALUES clause.

Example 5.3   Example 5.2 can be coded as follows:

```
INSERT INTO PATIENT
    (patname, patno, address, birthdate, sex)
    VALUES ('burton', '0002', NULL, NULL, 'm')
```

Example 5.4   Suppose we have a Cobol program similar the one in Figure 4.1 and our structure PATINFO contains all the values we want to insert. We can code the embedded INSERT statement as follows:

```
EXEC SQL
    INSERT INTO PATIENT
       (patname, patno, address, birthdate, sex, ssnum)
    VALUES ( :named, :id, :address, :birthdate, :sex, :socsec )
END-EXEC.
or
EXEC SQL
    INSERT INTO PATIENT
       (patname, patno, address, birthdate, sex, ssnum)
    VALUES (:patinfo)
END-EXEC.
```

When the INSERT statement is embedded in an application program, after each successful insertion, DB2 puts a value in the third field of SQLERRD, or SQLERRD(3), in the SQLCA to specify the number of rows inserted.

5.2.3 Inserting multiple rows

The INSERT statements we've seen so far allow us to insert only one row at a time. However, DB2 also allows us to insert one or more rows into a table with one INSERT statement by embedding a SELECT statement within it. The general format of the INSERT statement to add multiple rows to a table is:

```
INSERT INTO table name
    (column-name ...)
    SELECT statement ...
```

The SELECT statement is coded within an INSERT to select one or more rows from one or more tables to insert into the table specified in the INTO clause. The SELECT statement embedded in the INSERT statement is the same interactive SELECT statement that we use to retrieve data; the only exception is that we cannot use the ORDER BY clause.

Example 5.5   An application uses a table called PNAME which contains only PATNO and PATNAME. In order to insert a row for a patient with PATNO 0001, we need to code an INSERT statement as follows:

```
INSERT INTO pname
    (patno, patname)
  SELECT patient.patno, patient.patname
    FROM patient
    WHERE patient.patno = '0001'
```

The first INSERT rule says that the data types of the values in the VALUES clause or the data types of the columns in the enclosed SELECT statement must be compatible with the data types of the columns into which we're inserting data. In Example 5.1, it is invalid to code the INSERT statement as follows:

```
INSERT INTO PATIENT
    (patname, patno, address, birthdate, sex, ssnum)
    VALUES ('burton', 0002, '200 century boulevard',
      '800520', 'm', 586529443)
```

Because PATNO and SSNUM are defined as character fields, we cannot assign numeric values to them; the new values assigned to them must be enclosed in quotes. As mentioned in Chapter 2, each table should have a key with a unique value to identify the rows of the table. If a table is defined without a key field, we can insert as many duplicate rows as we want without errors. Each new row inserted is at the end of the table.

Example 5.6   Suppose our PATIENT table is created without a key field; after a statement in Example 5.1 is executed, a new row will be inserted as follows:

PATNAME	PATNO	ADDRESS	BIRTHDATE	SEX	SSNUM
smith	0001	123 first street	400320	m	111001111
doe	0010	225 wilshire boulevard	550912	m	221002222

PATNAME	PATNO	ADDRESS	BIRTHDATE	SEX	SSNUM
jackson	0005	654 soto street	541205	f	330113323
adams	0003	5674 sun-set street	400320	m	442134366
brown	0028	12 willow street	640213	f	343350945
johnson	0020	9534 valley boulevard	330814	m	348650973
parker	0017	7655 grand avenue	781112	f	689545853
lee	0042	7462 santa monica boulevard	450530	m	788575443
burton	0002	200 century boulevard	800520	m	586529443

On the other the hand, if a table is created with a unique key field, the rows inserted into the table will be placed in the order of the key field and DB2 will not allow us to insert a new row with the same key field since another row already exists in the table.

Example 5.7 This example shows the result of an execution of a statement in Example 5.1. Notice that the new row is inserted right after the first row in the table.

PATNAME	PATNO	ADDRESS	BIRTHDATE	SEX	SSNUM
smith	0001	123 first street	400320	m	111001111
burton	0002	200 century boulevard	800520	m	586529443
adams	0003	5674 sun-set street	400320	m	442134366
jackson	0005	654 soto street	541205	f	330113323
doe	0010	225 wilshire boulevard	550912	m	221002222

PATNAME	PATNO	ADDRESS	BIRTHDATE	SEX	SSNUM
parker	0017	7655 grand avenue	781112	f	689545853
johnson	0020	9534 valley boulevard	330814	m	348650973
brown	0028	12 willow street	640213	f	343350945
lee	0042	7462 santa monica boulevard	450530	m	788575443

The third INSERT rule says that the table name specified in the INTO clause of an INSERT statement cannot be the same as the table name(s) specified in the SELECT statement within it. In other words, we cannot insert new rows into the table we're selecting from; it is not valid to have an INSERT statement like this:

```
INSERT INTO patient
  SELECT *
    FROM patient
    WHERE patient.patno = '0001'
```

We've learned earlier that DB2 puts a lot of useful information in the SQLCA and we should always check the SQLCA after the execution of our SQL statement. The INSERT statement below shows four values of the SQLCODE that are common to INSERT statements. The −408 code is self-explanatory. It's never valid to have an insert value with a different data type than the existing column. We'd get the −407 code if we did not supply a value for a column defined as NOT NULL. A −117 return code means that the number of insert values is not the same as the number of columns in the INTO clause. The +100 return code indicates that the embedded SELECT in an INSERT statement returns no rows and the −121 return code means that a column is listed more than once in an INSERT statement.

SQLCODE

return code   Meaning

000   SUCCESSFUL INSERTION

+ 100   ROW NOT FOUND

− 117   THE NUMBER OF INSERT VALUES IS NOT THE SAME AS THE NUMBER OF OBJECT COLUMNS.

– 121	COLUMN column-name IS SPECIFIED MORE THAN ONCE.
– 407	AN INSERT VALUE IS NULL, BUT THE OBJECT COLUMN column-name CANNOT CONTAIN NULL. The actual column-name is returned in the SQLERRMC.
– 408	AN INSERT VALUE NOT COMPATIBLE WITH DATA TYPE OF ITS OBJECT COLUMN column-name. DB2 will return the actual column-name in the SQLERRMC field of the SQLCA.

5.3 Loading DB2 Tables

Loading refers to the process of entering a large amount of data into an empty table. Normally, a DB2 database is created to support one or more applications. But, before an application can be up and running, its database must contain real information and that is the result of a database load process. There are three ways to load data into DB2 tables and it is totally up to us to choose the method we want to use.

5.3.1 Three ways to load DB2 tables

Loading data into DB2 tables is usually more straightforward than updating or retrieving data from them. There are three ways we can load data into DB2 tables. We can use an SQL INSERT statement with an embedded SELECT statement to retrieve rows from other tables and insert them into our table, we can use an embedded INSERT statement within an application program to load our table, or we can use the DB2 LOAD utility. However, there is one requirement that all three approaches need: The table we are loading must already be created in the DB2 catalog. In deciding which approach to use, the thing to keep in mind is to try to use the approach which we find the easiest and which will do the job.

5.3.2 Using mass INSERT

The first approach is to use an embedded SELECT statement within an INSERT statement to retrieve multiple rows from one or more tables and insert them into an empty table. The INSERT statement to load a table looks exactly like the INSERT statement to insert a new row into an existing table. Example 5.8 shows an INSERT statement to load a sample table. We've seen how to code this statement earlier in this chapter. This is the format of the INSERT statement that we would use to load a DB2 table after we created it.

Example 5.8   Suppose we have a table named PATADM which contains IDNO, ADDATE, and DSDATE of all the patients who have been in the hospital since

1986. After defining it to DB2, we would use the following INSERT statement to load it:

```
INSERT INTO patadm
    (idno, addate,dsdate)
  SELECT visit.idno,visit.addate,visit.dsdate
    FROM VISIT
    WHERE visit.addate > '860000'
```

When using an embedded SELECT statement within an INSERT statement to load a new table or insert new rows into it, DB2 will insert the rows in the order in which it retrieves them; we cannot control the insertion sequence. This first approach is useful only if the data we want to load into our table already exist in other DB2 tables. It is particularly handy when we want to extract a subset of the data from one or more tables and combine it into a single table for testing purposes.

5.3.3 Using a load program

Although the first approach is the simplest of the three, there are several circumstances in which we cannot use that approach. The most common situation is that the data we want to load into our table come from a different medium (i.e., tape) or are in different formats. The second approach involves writing an application program with an embedded SQL INSERT statement to load our table. When using this approach, we can control the insertion sequence and the format and content of the data and can also select the input medium.

Figure 5.1 shows a sample load program written in Cobol. This sample is very similar to the retrieval program in Figure 4.1. With the exception of the SQL INSERT statement, we can use all the techniques used in the retrieval program. Notice that our load program does not perform any editing or validation on the input data before inserting them into the PATIENT table. It's a simple program used to load new rows into the PATIENT table. Rows of data are read from an input data set and the program moves the values into the corresponding variables in a host structure. The SQL INSERT statement is executed, and the program checks the SQLCODE value. The whole process is repeated until the end of the input data set. The program then prints out the number of records processed and the number of rows inserted.

The program in Figure 5.1 is used to illustrate the second approach in database loading. It does not include any editing routines, which are very important in maintaining data consistency in the database. When we use the second approach to load our table, the input data may come from different sources (i.e., tape) and be in any format. It is the function of the load program to decode or move the input data into

```
000010   ID DIVISION.
000020   PROGRAM-ID.  SAMPLE3.
000030   AUTHOR.  VIET G. TRAN.
000040   DATE-COMPILED.
000050   REMARKS.  THIS PROGRAM READS AN INPUT FILE CONTAINING PATIENT
000060             NAME, IDENTIFICATION NUMBERS, ADDRESS, BIRTHDATE AND,
000070             SOCIAL SECURITY NUMBER AND LOADS THE PATIENT TABLE.
000080
000090   ENVIRONMENT DIVISION.
000100
000110   CONFIGURATION SECTION.
000120   SOURCE-COMPUTER.  IBM-3090.
000130   OBJECT-COMPUTER.  IBM-3090.
000140   SPECIAL-NAMES.  C01 IS NEW-PAGE.
000150   INPUT-OUTPUT SECTION.
000160   FILE-CONTROL.
000170
000180       SELECT IDFILE
000190           ASSIGN TO UT-S-IDFILE.
000200
000210       SELECT OUTFILE
000220           ASSIGN TO UT-S-OUTFILE.
000230
000240   DATA DIVISION.
000250
000260   FILE SECTION.
000270
000280   FD  IDFILE
000290       LABEL RECORDS ARE STANDARD
000300       BLOCK CONTAINS 0 RECORDS
000310       RECORDING MODE IS F
000320       RECORD CONTAINS 80 CHARACTERS
000330       DATA RECORD IS ID-REC.
000340
000350   01  ID-REC                     PIC X(80).
000360
000370   FD  OUTFILE
000380       LABEL RECORDS ARE OMITTED
000390       BLOCK CONTAINS 0 RECORDS
000400       RECORDING MODE IS F
000410       RECORD CONTAINS 133 CHARACTERS
000420       DATA RECORD IS OUT-REC.
000430
000440   01  OUT-REC.
000450       05  OUT-CCTL               PIC X.
000460       05  OUT-PRT                PIC X(132).
000470
000480   WORKING-STORAGE SECTION.
000490
000500   01  WS-ID-REC.
000510       05  WS-NAME                PIC X(10).
000520       05  WS-ID                  PIC X(4).
000530       05  WS-ADDRESS             PIC X(30).
000540       05  WS-BIRTH               PIC X(6).
000550       05  WS-SEX                 PIC X(1).
000560       05  WS-SOCSEC              PIC X(9).
000570       05  FILLER                 PIC X(20).
000580
000590   01  PATINFO.
000600       05  NAME.
```

Fig. 5.1 PATIENT table load program.

```
000610              49  NAMEL              PIC S9(4) COMP.
000620              49  NAMED              PIC X(10) VALUE SPACES.
000630          05  ID                     PIC X(4).
000640          05  ADDRESS.
000650              49  ADDRESSL           PIC S9(4) COMP.
000660              49  ADDRESSD           PIC X(30) VALUE SPACES.
000670          05  BIRTHDATE              PIC X(6).
000680          05  SEX                    PIC X(1).
000690          05  SOCSEC                 PIC X(9).
000700
000710  01  WORK-FIELDS.
000720          05  INREC                  PIC 9(3) VALUE 0.
000730          05  OUTREC                 PIC 9(3) VALUE 0.
000740
000750  01  STATUS-SWITCHES.
000760          05  EOF-SWITCH             PIC X VALUE '0'.
000770              88  EOF                VALUE '1'.
000780
000790  01  DETAIL.
000800          05  FILLER                 PIC X(5)  VALUE SPACES.
000810          05  MSSG                   PIC X(30).
000820          05  FILLER                 PIC X(1)  VALUE SPACE.
000830          05  RCOUNT                 PIC 9(3).
000840          05  FILLER                 PIC X(41) VALUE SPACES.
000850
000860          EXEC SQL DECLARE PATIENT TABLE
000870                  (PATNAME    VARCHAR(10)   NOT NULL,
000880                   PATNO      CHAR(4)        NOT NULL,
000890                   ADDRESS    VARCHAR(30),
000900                   BIRTHDATE  CHAR(6),
000910                   SEX        CHAR(1),
000920                   SSNUM      CHAR(9)        NOT NULL WITH DEFAULT)
000930              END-EXEC.
000940
000950          EXEC SQL INCLUDE SQLCA END-EXEC.
000960
000970          EJECT
000980  PROCEDURE DIVISION.
000990
001000          PERFORM 0000-INITIALIZE.
001010
001020          READ IDFILE INTO WS-ID-REC
001030                      AT END MOVE '1' TO EOF-SWITCH.
001040          PERFORM 1000-PROCESS-INPUT UNTIL EOF.
001050          PERFORM 3000-TERMINATE.
001060
001070          GOBACK.
001080
001090  0000-INITIALIZE.
001100  *--------------
001110
001120          OPEN INPUT  IDFILE
001130               OUTPUT OUTFILE.
001140
001150          MOVE '0'    TO EOF-SWITCH.
001160          MOVE SPACES TO OUT-PRT.
001170
001180  1000-PROCESS-INPUT.
001190  *------------------
001200
```

Fig. 5.1   *(Continued)*

```
001210         MOVE SPACES      TO NAMED.
001220         MOVE SPACES      TO ADDRESSD.
001230         ADD 1 TO INREC.
001240
001250         UNSTRING WS-NAME DELIMITED BY '.'
001260             INTO NAMED COUNT IN NAMEL.
001270
001280         UNSTRING WS-ADDRESS DELIMITED BY '.'
001290             INTO ADDRESSD COUNT IN ADDRESSL.
001300
001310         MOVE   WS-ID     TO ID.
001320         MOVE   WS-BIRTH  TO BIRTHDATE.
001330         MOVE   WS-SEX    TO SEX.
001340         MOVE   WS-SOCSEC TO SOCSEC.
001350
001360         EXEC SQL INSERT INTO PATIENT
001370             VALUES (:PATINFO)
001380             END-EXEC.
001390
001400         IF SQLCODE EQUAL TO ZERO
001410             ADD 1 TO OUTREC.
001420
001430         READ IDFILE INTO WS-ID-REC
001440             AT END MOVE '1' TO EOF-SWITCH.
001450
001460     3000-TERMINATE.
001470 *--------------
001480
001490         MOVE '***** TOTAL RECORDS READ      :' TO MSSG.
001500         MOVE INREC       TO   RCOUNT.
001510         MOVE DETAIL      TO   OUT-PRT.
001520         WRITE OUT-REC AFTER ADVANCING 1.
001530
001540         MOVE '***** TOTAL RECORDS INSERTED :' TO MSSG.
001550         MOVE OUTREC      TO   RCOUNT.
001560         MOVE DETAIL      TO   OUT-PRT.
001570         WRITE OUT-REC AFTER ADVANCING 1.
001580
001590         CLOSE IDFILE
001600             OUTFILE.
```

Fig. 5.1   *(Continued)*

columns of each row to be inserted. The patient name and address from the input file are delimited with a period (.).

5.3.4 Using DB2 LOAD utility

The third approach is probably the fastest way to load data into one or more tables. This approach uses a DB2 utility LOAD. DB2 supplies us with a set of utilities used for database maintenance purposes. The DBA is usually the person who most often uses these utilities. In order to illustrate the third approach in database loading, the LOAD utility is discussed separately in this chapter. The LOAD utility is a very powerful utility and it is used to load data into DB2 tables from sequential data sets.

The LOAD utility is similar to an SQL statement in the way that it contains multiple clauses to allow us to specify the options we want to use in the load process. However, like all DB2 utilities, it cannot be used interactively and must be run as a TSO batch job. There are four ways to invoke DB2 utilities. Readers should refer to their installation manuals for information about how to invoke DB2 utilities. Example 5.9 shows one way to invoke a DB2 utility by using the supplied Job Control Language (JCL) procedure called DSNUPROC.

Example 5.9   The following is a sample TSO job stream which uses the supplied procedure DSNUPROC to invoke a DB2 utility. This job stream contains a sample LOAD statement we would use to load our PATIENT table. 1

```
//LA#TEST JOB USER = TEST,MSGCLASS = A
//STEP1 EXEC DSNUPROC,SIZE = 2048K,SYSTEM = DSN,UID = TESTJOB
//SYSUT1 DD UNIT = SYSDA,SPACE = (CYL,(20,10))
//SORTLIB DD DSN = SYS1.SORTLIB,DISP = SHR
//SORTWK01 DD UNIT = SYSDA,SPACE = (CYL,(20,10))
//SORTWK02 DD UNIT = SYSDA,SPACE = (CYL,(20,10))
//SORTWK03 DD UNIT = SYSDA,SPACE = (CYL,(20,10))
//SORTWK04 DD UNIT = SYSDA,SPACE = (CYL,(20,10))
//SYSREC DD DSN = TEST.PATIENT.DATA,DISP = SHR
//SYSIN DD *
  LOAD DATA INDDN(SYSREC)
    RESUME NO
    WORKDDN(SYSUT1)
    INTO TABLE TEST.PATIENT
/*
```

Here is an explanation of the code:

The EXEC card invokes the DSNUPROC procedure with an execution area region size of 2048K, a DB2 subsystem named DSN, and a job identifier named TESTJOB.

The SYSUT1 card specifies the temporary work file for the LOAD utility.

The SORTLIB card points to the library in which the sort load module resides.

The SORTWK01-04 specifies the work files for sorting. The SYSREC card defines the LOAD input file.

The SYSIN card specifies the LOAD input statement.

In the LOAD statement, the key expression RESUME NO means that the table must be empty before any data can be loaded. If we wanted to add new records to the existing data, we would use the key expression RESUME YES. We can also tell DB2 to replace the existing data with the new data by using the key expression RESUME NO REPLACE. We can also specify a data set for DB2 to store records that are not loaded for any reason. In that case, we will need to add one more card to the job stream and one more key expression to the LOAD statement in Example 5.9:

```
//LA#TEST JOB USER = TEST,MSGCLASS = A
// ...           ..    ...
// ...           ..    ...
// ...           ..    ...
// ...           ..    ...
//SYSREC    DD    DSN = TEST.PATIENT.DATA,DISP = SHR
//SYSDISC   DD    DSN = TEST.PATIENT.REJECT,DISP(OLD,CATLG,DELETE),
//               UNIT - DISK,SPACE = (CYL,(10,2),RLSE),
//               DCB = (RECFM = VB,LRECL = 68,BLKSIZE = 6800)
//SYSIN     D     *
LOAD DATA INDDN(SYSREC)
    RESUME NO
    WORKDDN(SYSUT1)
    DISCARDDN(SYSDISC)
    INTO TABLE TEST.PATIENT
/*
```

As in an SQL statement, we can use the keyword WHEN in the LOAD statement to specify a condition that the input records must satisfy in order to be loaded. Any input records that do not satisfy the condition will be written out of the data set specified in the DISCARDDN clause if there is one defined in the job stream.

Example 5.10 The following shows a LOAD statement that loads all the male patients' records into the PATIENT table:

```
LOAD DATA INDDN(SYSREC)
    RESUME NO
    WORKDDN(SYSUT1)
    DISCARDDN(SYSDISC)
    INTO TABLE TEST.PATIENT
    WHEN sex = 'M'
```

All the above LOAD statements assume that the order of the fields in the input records must correspond to the order of the columns defined for PATIENT table. Sometimes the sequence of the fields in the input data set is not the same as the sequence of the columns in the table to be loaded. In the second approach, we can easily overcome this problem by moving the input values into the correct variables in the host structure before issuing an SQL INSERT statement. When using the LOAD utility, we can also specify the position of each field in the input record by using the field-specification option. Example 5.11 shows a LOAD statement using the field-specification option.

Example 5.11 Suppose the input record to our LOAD statement has the following layout:

PATNO	BIRTH-DATE	SEX	SSNUM	nn	PATNAME	nn	ADDRESS

```
1       4 5        10 11 11 12      20 21 23               33 35
```

Each field in the input record has a fixed length, except PATNAME and ADDRESS, which are varying lengths. Their lengths are determined by the 2-byte field in positions 21 and 33, respectively. The following is a LOAD statement which uses the field-specification option to load the above record type into the PATIENT table:

```
LOAD DATA INDDN(SYSREC)
    RESUME NO
    WORKDDN(SYSUT1)
    DISCARDDN(SYSDISC)
    INTO TABLE TEST.PATIENT
    (patno     POSITION(1:4)     char(4),
    birthdate  POSITION(5:10)    char(6),
    sex        POSITION(11:11)   char(1),
    ssnum      POSITION(12:20)   char(9),
    patname    POSITION(21)      varchar(10),
    address    POSITION(33)      varchar(30) )
```

The keyword POSITION is always followed by a pair of parentheses which contain a starting position and an ending position separated by a colon. For a varying-length column, the starting position must point to the 2-byte field that specifies the length of that column and the ending position is not used by DB2. The *IBM Database2 Reference Manual* has a section that describes all the available features of the LOAD utility. Readers can consult that section if additional information about the LOAD utility is desired.

6

Updating and Deleting

In any complete database management system (DBMS) we find facilities to delete unwanted data and update existing data with current information. In other words, database maintenance is always a major function in any DBMS. We've learned how to define, retrieve, and load DB2 tables in previous chapters. In this chapter, we shall learn how to delete and update existing rows in a table. We shall also see how to delete and update our DB2 table design.

6.1 Updating and Deleting Rows in a Table

Updating or deleting one or more rows in a table requires us to use the SQL UPDATE or DELETE statement. There are two types of UPDATE and DELETE statements. The first type can be used interactively or can be embedded within an application program; the second type must be embedded within an application program and used with a CURSOR statement.

6.2 The UPDATE Statement

The SQL UPDATE statement is used to modify the values of column(s) in one or more rows in a table. We can only update one table at a time with a single UPDATE statement. Like other SQL statements, the UPDATE statement must start with the key expression EXEC SQL and end with a host language delimiter when it is embedded within an application program. The table name specified in the UPDATE statement must be already defined in the DB2 catalog. The general format of the UPDATE statement is shown below; it can be issued interactively or can be embedded within an application.

```
UPDATE table name
  SET    column-name  =  expression ,
         column-name  =  NULL ,
         . . .        .  . . .
         . . .        .  . . .
WHERE condition
```

6.2.1 The SET clause

The SET clause in an UPDATE statement is used to list the column names we want to update and their new updated values. The column names cannot be listed more than once and must belong to the table specified. Each expression assigned to a column can be a constant, a column name, NULL, USER, or any arithmetic expression which does not contain a function. When an expression contains a column name, it cannot be a long string column. DB2 will use the value of the column before it gets updated to assign to the target column. The new value to be assigned to each column must be compatible with the data type of that column. In other words, we cannot update a character string column with a numeric value or assign a NULL value to a character string column that does not accept NULL value.

6.2.2 The WHERE clause

As in a SELECT statement, the WHERE clause is used to specify one or more conditions to limit the selection to only rows that satisfy the search criteria.

Example 6.1   The following will correct the social security number and the birth date of patient 0001:

```
UPDATE test.patient
  SET ssnum    = '111001110',
    birthdate = '400322'
WHERE patno = '0001'
```

Before the update, the information was:

PATNAME	PATNO	ADDRESS	BIRTHDATE	SEX	SSNUM
smith	0001	123 first street	400320	m	111001111

After the update, it is:

PATNAME	PATNO	ADDRESS	BIRTHDATE	SEX	SSNUM
smith	0001	123 first street	400322	m	111001110

Example 6.2   This code will increase the salary of all physicians in our PHY-SICIAN table by 10 percent:

```
UPDATE test.physician
  SET salary   = salary + (salary *0.1)
```

After the above statement is executed, our PHYSICIAN table in Figure 2.2 will look like this:

PHYNAME	PHYNO	DEPARTMENT	HIREDATE	SALARY
stern	345	general medicine	750312	48092.00
mitchum	867	obstetrics	661211	64636.00
miller	234	dermatology	670423	65637.00
thompson	432	neurology	760322	84194.00
burton	479	cardiology	470506	94364.60
jones	916	pediatrics	731205	54623.80
stein	612	general medicine	801115	48023.80

We can see that the SQL UPDATE statement is a very powerful statement; we can use it to update one or more rows in a table or the whole table. However, DB2 will not update any rows if it finds an error in the UPDATE statement.

6.2.3 The WHERE CURRENT OF clause

The second type of UPDATE statement is called the cursor-controlled UPDATE statement. It must be embedded within an application program and used with a CURSOR statement. The format of this UPDATE statement looks exactly like the first one with one exception: We must use the WHERE CURRENT OF clause instead of the regular WHERE clause. The WHERE CURRENT OF clause is used to specify the row we want to update, which is where a cursor is positioned. The general format of the second UPDATE statement is as follows:.

```
UPDATE table name
  SET    column-name = expression ,
         column-name = NULL ,
         ...         . ...
         ...         . ...
WHERE CURRENT OF cursor name
```

Example 6.3   Instead of showing a whole program as in Figure 4.2, we will only show the SQL statements needed to use a cursor-controlled update statement in an application program. We will use the same program as in Figure 4.2, but in this example, our program will update the VISIT table. All the SQL statements are numbered for easy reference. The code is:

```
ID DIVISION.
    ...
```

```
       . . .
    ENVIRONMENT DIVISION.
       . . .
       . . .
    DATA DIVISION.
       . . .
       . . .
    WORKING-STORAGE SECTION.
    . . .
    . . .
1. EXEC SQL DECLARE VISIT TABLE
         ( IDNO        CHAR( 4 )        NOT NULL,
           SEQUN       CHAR( 3 )        NOT NULL,
           MDNO        CHAR( 3 )        NOT NULL,
           ADDATE      CHAR( 6 )        NOT NULL,
           DSDATE      CHAR( 6 )        ,
           DIAGNOSIS   VARCHAR( 20 )    NOT NULL WITH DEFAULT )
      END-EXEC.
       . . .
       . . .
2.  EXEC SQL INCLUDE SQLCA END-EXEC.
3.  EXEC SQL DECLARE PVISIT CURSOR FOR
       SELECT *
       FROM VISIT
       WHERE IDNO = :IDNUM
       FOR UPDATE OF DSDATE, DIAGNOSIS
      END-EXEC.
PROCEDURE DIVISION.
       . . .
       . . .
    . . . read an input record containing a patient id into a host
    variable
4.  EXEC SQL OPEN PVISIT END-EXEC.
5.  EXEC SQL FETCH PVISIT INTO :VISITINFO END-EXEC.
       . . .
    . . . for each row retrieved, update the discharge date and patient
 -  diagnosis with values in host variables.
       . . .
6.  EXEC SQL UPDATE VISIT
         SET DSDATE    = :REAL-DATE ,
           DIAGNOSIS = :DIAG
         WHERE CURRENT OF PVISIT
       END-EXEC.
       . . .
    . . . loop back to get next row.
       . . .
7.  EXEC SQL CLOSE PVISIT END-EXEC.
       . . .
    . . . loop back to read next input record.
       . . .
```

The first and second SQL statements are simple; they are exactly the same as in a retrieval program. The third SQL statement is used to declare a cursor named PVISIT and is similar to the one in Figure 4.2 with only two exceptions. First, the SELECT statement cannot contain the keyword DISTINCT, any function (MIN, MAX, COUNT, etc.), a GROUP BY clause, a HAVING clause, or an ORDER BY clause. There is an additional clause FOR UPDATE OF...which is used to tell DB2 the name of each column we plan to update. Each column we want to update must be specified in the FOR UPDATE OF...clause. A column name does not have to be in the result table before we can update it, but it must be in the FOR UPDATE OF...clause.

The fourth and fifth SQL statements open the cursor and retrieve a row into a host structure. The sixth SQL statement is a cursor-controlled update statement; it updates the discharge date and the patient diagnosis. The WHERE CURRENT OF clause is used to tell DB2 the current row we want to update. The last SQL statement is used to close the PVISIT cursor. The cursor-controlled UPDATE statement is particularly useful when we want to retrieve a row and examine it before updating it.

Listed below are some SQLCODE return codes that can be returned as a result of an UPDATE statement. The 000 code always means a successful execution. The +100 means that DB2 cannot find any row that satisfies the selection criteria for update. The -121 code is returned if a column name is specified more than once in the SET clause. We'd get the -407 code if we tried to update a column defined as NOT NULL with a NULL value. The -408 code tells us that the object column and the updated value have different data types. The -503 code is returned if we try to update a column that is not specified in the FOR UPDATE clause.

SQLCODE
return code | Meaning

SQLCODE return code	Meaning
000	STATEMENT EXECUTED SUCCESSFULLY; field SQLERRD(3) contains the number of rows updated.
+100	NO ROW FOUND TO BE UPDATED IN AN UPDATE STATEMENT.
-121	COLUMN column-name IS SPECIFIED MORE THAN ONCE.
-407	AN UPDATE VALUE IS NULL, BUT THE OBJECT COLUMN column-name CANNOT CONTAIN NULL.

-408   AN UPDATE VALUE NOT COMPATIBLE WITH DATA
              TYPE OF ITS OBJECT COLUMN column-name.
-503   COLUMN CANNOT BE UPDATED BECAUSE IT IS NOT
              SPECIFIED IN THE FOR UPDATE CLAUSE.

6.3   The DELETE Statement

The SQL DELETE statement is used to remove one or more whole rows from a table. The DELETE statement cannot delete a single column in a row. In a single DELETE statement, we can only delete rows from one table. Like an UPDATE statement, the DELETE statement can be used interactively or embedded within an application program. The general format of an SQL DELETE statement is as follows:

```
DELETE table name    WHERE condition
```

or

```
DELETE table name
    WHERE CURRENT OF cursor name
```

The first SQL DELETE statement can be issued interactively or can be embedded within an application program. The second DELETE statement is a cursor-control DELETE statement. It must be used with a CURSOR statement and embedded within an application program. The syntax of the WHERE clause and the WHERE CURRENT OF clause in a DELETE statement is the same as in an UPDATE statement.

Example 6.4   We want to delete all patient visits prior to 1985.

```
DELETE test.visit
    WHERE addate < '850101'
```

We must be very careful when using the first DELETE statement because it is a very powerful statement. If it is used without the WHERE clause, it can remove all the rows from a table.

Example 6.5   As in Example 6.4, suppose we want to use the cursor-controlled DELETE statement in an application program; we would use the following:

```
ID DIVISION.
    . . .
    . . .
ENVIRONMENT DIVISION.
    . . .
    . . .
DATA DIVISION.
    . . .
    . . .
```

```
WORKING-STORAGE SECTION.
    . . .
    . . .
    EXEC SQL DECLARE VISIT TABLE
        ( IDNO      CHAR( 4 )      NOT NULL,
          SEQUN     CHAR( 3 )      NOT NULL,
          MDNO      CHAR( 3 )      NOT NULL,
          ADDATE    CHAR( 6 )      NOT NULL,
          DSDATE    CHAR( 6 )      ,
          DIAGNOSIS VARCHAR( 20 )  NOT NULL WITH DEFAULT )
        END-EXEC.
    . . .
    . . .
    EXEC SQL INCLUDE SQLCA END-EXEC.
    EXEC SQL DECLARE PVISIT CURSOR FOR
            SELECT *
            FROM VISIT
            WHERE ADDATE  <  '850101'
            END-EXEC.
PROCEDURE DIVISION.
    . . .
    . . .
    EXEC SQL OPEN PVISIT END-EXEC.
    EXEC SQL FETCH PVISIT INTO :VISITINFO END-EXEC.
    . . .
    . . . delete each row retrieved
    . . .
    EXEC SQL DELETE VISIT
        WHERE CURRENT OF PVISIT
      END-EXEC.
    . . .
    . . . loop back to get next row.
    . . .
    EXEC SQL CLOSE PVISIT END-EXEC.
    . . .
    . . .
```

Two SQL return codes that we most often get as a result of a DE-
LETE statement are 000 and +100. The SQLCODE with a value 000
means that the DELETE statement has been successfully executed
and the number of rows deleted is contained in field SQLERRD(3). A
+100 return code means that no row has been deleted.

6.4 Modifying and Deleting a Database Design

A database design is always subject to changes at any installation. It
does not matter what environment we're in; changes to a database design always occur. Those changes can result from the following:

1. Current application programs contain some problems or need to be enhanced and a database design change is required to support the fixes or the changes.

2. New applications need to be incorporated into the existing environment.

3. Some applications are installed in phases and each phase requires some modification to our database design.

4. A database design change is needed to improve system performance.

Changes are not the only things that can happen to a database design. In the worst case, if a database is poorly designed, it has to be deleted completely. We've seen in Chapter 3 how to create our tables after completing our database design. In this chapter we'll see how to change a table design or delete it completely if we are not satisfied with it. The two expressions "database design" and "table design" are used interchangeably because, in a DB2 environment, a database is just a collection of tables.

6.5   The ALTER Statement

The SQL ALTER statement is used to change a DB2 object. A DB2 object is defined as a table, a table space, a database, an index, etc. We will discuss other DB2 objects in Chapter 7. Since the ALTER statement can be used to manipulate different DB2 objects, there is one form of the ALTER statement for each DB2 object that we want to modify.

6.5.1   The ALTER TABLE statement

The ALTER TABLE statement is used to modify the definition of a table. With this statement, we can only add a column to a table, but we cannot remove one. The new column added will be to the right of the last column in a table. Sometimes we just want to add a validation routine to a table; we can also do that with the ALTER TABLE statement. The general format of the SQL ALTER TABLE is as follows; like other SQL statements, it can be used interactively or embedded within an application program:

```
ALTER TABLE table-name
    ADD column-name  data-type
    VALIDPROC program-name | NULL
```

Example 6.6   We want to add a new column called BIRTHDATE to our PHYSICIAN table; it contains the physicians' birth dates.

The following shows how we do it:

```
ALTER TABLE test.physician
   ADD birthdate  char(6)
```

When specifying the data type of the new column in the ADD clause, we cannot specify NOT NULL but we can specify NOT NULL WITH DEFAULT. We can also specify FIELDPROC if we want to use a field procedure for the new column. When the above ALTER TABLE statement is executed, the existing data within the PHYSICIAN table remain unchanged; only the table description gets changed. Each existing row in the PHYSICIAN table will have a default value as the value for the new column. We've seen in Chapter 3 that DB2 keeps all the information we define to it in the DB2 catalog. Every time a change is made to a table using an ALTER TABLE statement, the information about that table in the DB2 catalog is also updated to reflect the change. We can only add one column with a single ALTER TABLE statement. If more than one column needs to be added to a table, each column requires a separate ALTER statement.

Example 6.7   In this example, we want to use a validation routine called EDITTAB for the PHYSICIAN table. It looks like this:

```
ALTER TABLE test.physician
   VALIDPROC edittab
```

When we issue the above SQL ALTER TABLE statement, if our PHYSICIAN table does not have any validation routine associated with it, DB2 will connect EDITTAB to our PHYSICIAN Table. If our PHYSICIAN table already has a validation routine associated with it, DB2 will disconnect the old routine and connect the new one because only one validation routine can be active at any one time. Since the validation routine is only invoked when a row is updated or inserted into a table, all the existing rows in our PHYSICIAN table are not validated by the new routine. A data inconsistency problem in a table may occur when we try to add or change a new validation routine. In order to avoid this problem, we can unload all the existing rows from our PHYSICIAN table to a tape and use it to reload our table with the DB2 LOAD utility. This way, all the rows in our PHYSICIAN table that pass the new validation routine will be loaded and the rest will be rejected.

Example 6.8   The following ALTER TABLE statement is an example of how to add a new column to and disconnect an existing validation from the PHYSICIAN table:

```
ALTER TABLE test.physician
   ADD sex    char(1) NOT NULL WITH DEFAULT
   VALIDPROC NULL
```

The keyword NULL in the VALIDPROC clause is used to disconnect a validation routine. After the above statement is executed, whenever a row is updated or inserted, DB2 will no longer invoke the validation routine.

6.6 The DROP Statement

We use the SQL DROP statement to delete a DB2 object. If an object is deleted, its definition in the DB2 catalog is also deleted and all the application programs that reference that object are no longer valid. Like the ALTER statement described in Section 6.5, the DROP statement can be used to delete different types of DB2 objects. The DROP statement can be used interactively or it can be embedded in an application program.

6.6.1 The DROP TABLE statement

The SQL DROP TABLE statement deletes a DB2 table. Whenever a table is deleted, all its data are also lost. We've seen in Chapter 3 that if we do not specify an existing table space when we create our table, DB2 will implicitly create a table space for our table. Thus, when we drop our table, its table space is also dropped if it was implicitly created. The general format of the SQL DROP TABLE statement is as follows:

```
DROP TABLE table-name
```

The table name can be any existing table in the DB2 catalog other than the DB2 catalog tables.

Example 6.9   In this example we want to delete a table named TEST.EMPLOYEE; we would do so as follows:

```
DROP TABLE test.employee
```

Sometimes there are changes we want to make to a DB2 table which cannot be done with an ALTER statement. To incorporate such changes, we have to drop the table and recreate it. For instance, we want to delete the new column we added to our PHYSICIAN table in Example 6.8, we want to change the attribute of column DIAGNOSIS from VARCHAR(20) to VARCHAR(30), or we want the column ADDATE to be able to accept NULL values. These changes must be made by dropping the table and recreating it; they cannot be made with an ALTER statement.

6.6.2   The DROP SYNONYM statement

The SQL DROP SYNONYM statement is used to delete a synonym we've created. The general format is as follows:

```
DROP SYNONYM synonym
```

Example 6.10   Delete the synonym named DEPARTMENT as follows:

```
DROP SYNONYM department
```

DB2 Objects Spaces

Before going into the advanced features of DB2, we should talk about DB2 objects spaces, which will help us better understand the advanced topics in later chapters. Normally, the application programmer or the user does not need to be concerned with the physical storage of a database or a table. It is normally determined by the systems programmer or the DBA. In this chapter, we'll be talking a little bit about the physical structure of DB2 objects. We will discuss those topics that are of the most interest to us as a user or an application programmer.

7.1 Virtual Storage Access Method

Since DB2 employs Virtual Storage Access Method (VSAM) data sets to store data, in this section we'll give a brief overview of the functions and characteristics of the access method that DB2 uses. VSAM is a comprehensive service method that comprises two functions: Record Management and Catalog Management.

7.1.1 The Record Management function

The Record Management function organizes fixed- and variable-length records into three types of data sets on direct access storage devices (DASD). A Key-Sequenced Data Set (KSDS) is a VSAM file in which the records are ordered in key sequence. An Entry-Sequenced Data Set (ESDS) is a VSAM file in which the records are organized in the sequence in which they are written on the file, and in a Relative-Record Data Set (RRDS) the records are stored by their relative record number or slot. Each VSAM data set must be defined to VSAM before it can be used. VSAM provides us with a set of commands and a ser-

vice program called the Access Method Services to define and manipulate VSAM data sets.

7.1.2 The Catalog Management function

The Catalog Management function maintains all the information
about each data set defined to VSAM in a catalog. A catalog is a KSDS
data set that contains all the VSAM data set information and the volume to locate them, and it controls access to those data sets.

7.2 Storage Groups

In a DASD, the term "volume" refers to the storage device or disk
pack served by an access mechanism (read/write mechanism). A volume can be permanently mounted or mounted by the operator when
requested. Each volume contains a serial number that the operating
system reads to ensure that the correct volume is mounted. To give us
an idea how much data a volume can hold, an IBM 3380 DASD is usually shipped in a box which contains four volumes. For a single- ·
density 3380 device, each volume can hold up 630.2 million bytes, and
of course, a volume in a double-density 3380 device will hold twice
that much. Thus, if we consider a 3380 device as a unit with four volumes, it can hold up 10.08 billion bytes.

A storage group is a set of DASD volumes that physically holds DB2
data. All the volumes in a storage group must belong to the same device type. In other words, if a storage group is defined to use 3380-type
volumes, all of its volumes must be the same type. Since DB2 uses
VSAM data sets to store its data, all the volumes in a DB2 storage
group are controlled by a VSAM catalog. The maximum number of
volumes that a storage group can have is 133.

7.2.1 The CREATE STOGROUP statement

SQL CREATE STOGROUP is used to define a storage group. As for
other DB2 objects, DB2 keeps all the information about each storage
group defined to it in the DB2 catalog. This statement can be used interactively or can be embedded within an application. The general format of the CREATE STOGROUP is as follows:

```
CREATE STOGROUP storage-group-name
    VOLUMES ( volume-serial-number ,
                 . . .              ,
        volume-serial-number )
    VCAT vsam-catalog-name
    PASSWORD password
```

We must assign a unique name to each storage group we define to DB2. Each name must start with an alpha character followed by zero or more alphanumeric characters or underscores up to eight characters. A DB2 reserved word cannot be used as a storage name. We specify one or more volume serial numbers in the VOLUMES clause. Volume serial numbers must be separated by a comma and contain at most six characters. We cannot specify more than 133 volumes for a single storage group. But more than one storage group can share one volume. We give the name of the VSAM catalog in the VCAT clause and it must not have more than eight characters. If we have a password to be used to access the VSAM catalog, we specify it in the PASSWORD clause. Otherwise, DB2 will not use any password to access the VSAM catalog. If we do not want to define our own storage group, we can always use the default storage SYSDEFLT that was defined upon installation of DB2.

Example 7.1   The following statements define two storage groups that have a common volume (i.e., CDP135):

```
CREATE STOGROUP tst100
    VOLUMES ( cdp125,cdp130,cdp135 )
    VCAT    chcat1
    PASSWORD  secret1

CREATE STOGROUP tst200
  VOLUMES ( cdp135,cdp140,cdp145 )
  VCAT chcat2
  PASSWORD secret2

CREATE STOGROUP tst200 VOLUMES ( cdp135,cdp140,cdp145 ) VCAT chcat2
PASSWORD secret2
```

7.2.2 The ALTER STOGROUP statement

From time to time, as more applications get developed, we need to go in and modify the definition of a storage group to meet the new external storage requirements. The SQL ALTER STOGROUP statement allows us to modify the DASD volumes in a storage group. One or more volumes can be added to or removed from a storage group with an ALTER STOGROUP statement. The general format of the ALTER STOGROUP is as follows:

```
ALTER STOGROUP storage-group-name
      PASSWORD password
      ADD VOLUMES ( volume-serial-number ,
                  . . .                  ,
                  volume-serial-number )
    REMOVE VOLUMES ( volume-serial-number ,
                  . . .                  ,
                  volume-serial-number )
```

The ALTER STOGROUP statement can be executed interactively or can be embedded within an application. Like the CREATE STOGROUP statement, we need to specify the password if there is one in the PASSWORD clause. When we add new volumes to a storage group, the new volumes must be of the same device type as the existing ones. If we remove volumes from a storage group, all the existing DB2 data residing on those volumes will remain intact. DB2 just will not use those volumes again for future space allocation for that particular storage group.

Example 7.2   The following adds volumes CDP150 and CDP155 to storage group TST100 and removes volumes CDP135, CDP140 from storage group TST200 and adds volume CDP160 to it:

```
ALTER STOGROUP tst100
    PASSWORD secret1
    ADD VOLUMES ( cdp150,cdp155 )

ALTER STOGROUP tst200
 PASSWORD secret2
 ADD VOLUMES ( cdp160 )
REMOVE VOLUMES ( cdp135,cdp140 )
```

7.2.3 The DROP STOGROUP statement

We can delete a storage group using the SQL DROP STOGROUP statement. The storage group we want to drop must already be defined in the DB2 catalog and must not be the default storage group SYSDEFLT. We also cannot delete a storage group that has already been used (i.e., contains DB2 data). The DROP STOGROUP statement only allows us to drop one storage group at a time; its format is:

```
DROP STOGROUP storage-group-name
```

7.3 Databases

In any database environment, data associated with one or more applications are grouped in one database. Similarly, in a DB2 environment, a database consists of all the DB2 objects (i.e., tables, etc.) that pertain to one or more applications.

7.3.1 The CREATE DATABASE statement

The SQL CREATE DATABASE statement defines a database to DB2. It has the following format:

```
CREATE DATABASE  database-name
        STOGROUP  storage-group-name
        BUFFERPOOL   BP0 or BP1 or BP2 or BP32K
```

When we create a database, we give it a unique name. The name we use must start with an alpha character followed by zero or more alphanumeric characters or underscores up to eight characters. We cannot use a reserved word for a database name or start a database name with the string DSNDB. The storage group to be used is specified in the STOGROUP clause. If the STOGROUP clause is not used, DB2 will use the default storage group SYSDEFLT.

The physical storage that holds data for a DB2 table is usually divided into small sections called "pages." The size of each page is usually about 4096 bytes (4K) or 32,768 bytes (32K), depending on the installation. Thus, each page will hold more than one row of data from a table. When a table row is referenced in an application program, DB2 goes out and copies the page containing that row into an area of main storage called the "buffer pool." If another row from the same page is referenced, DB2 does not have to go out to bring that page into memory because it is already residing in the buffer pool. By the same token, if an application modifies data in a row, the data in that row in the buffer pool is modified and then written back to the external storage. The buffer pool serves as a scratch pad for DB2 to perform work requested by applications. The choice of the buffer pool is specified in the BUFFERPOOL clause and there are four of them: BP0, BP1, BP2, and BP32K. The size of each buffer pool is specified upon installation of DB2. Choosing the buffer pool and its size may affect the performance of an application; thus, its choice is usually the task of a systems programmer or the DBA. DB2 will use the default buffer pool BP0 if the BUFFERPOOL clause is not specified in a CREATE DATABASE statement.

Like the storage group, there is a default database that we can use if we want to create our own database. The default database is called DSNDB04.

Example 7.3   Database DBTST100 is created using storage group TST100 and buffer pool BP1, and database DBTST200 is created using storage group SYSDEFLT and buffer pool BP0 as follows:

```
CREATE DATABASE dbtst100
    STOGROUP tst100
    BUFFERPOOL bp1
CREATE DATABASE dbtst200
```

7.3.2   The DROP DATABASE statement

The SQL ALTER statement does not allow us to change databases. The only way we can modify a database is to delete it and redefine it. We can use the SQL DROP DATABASE to drop a database other than any of the default databases such as DSNDB04, DSNDB06, and DSNDB07. The DROP DATABASE statement is used as follows:

```
DROP DATABASE database-name
```

The DROP DATABASE statement has a cascading effect that we must remember. When we delete a database, all the objects that belong to that database are also deleted (e.g., tables). Normally, we only use the DROP DATABASE statement when we need to change the default storage group or buffer pool of a database.

7.4   Table Spaces

DB2 table spaces are VSAM Entry-Sequenced Data Sets (ESDS) within a database that hold DB2 table data. Each table space can have from 1 to 64 ESDS and contain one or more tables. The size of each table space is limited to 64,000,000,000 bytes (64 gigabytes). As we've seen in earlier sections, data from each table space are retrieved or written in pages. Normally, when we create or update a table, DB2 manages the external storage requirements for us. This involves defining the necessary VSAM data sets, extending them when needed, or deleting the unnecessary ones.

As we've seen in Chapter 3, if we do not create our own table space, DB2 will create one for us and manage it. We can also create our table space using the SQL CREATE TABLESPACE statement and let DB2 manage it. A table space can be either simple or partitioned. When DB2 implicitly creates a table space for us, it uses all the default options of the CREATE TABLESPACE statement and creates a simple table space. But when we explicitly create our own table space, we can either make it simple or partitioned.

The main difference between a simple and a partitioned table space is as follows: A simple table space can contain more than one table and must belong to a single storage group. On the other hand, a partitioned table space can only contain one table and is divided into partitions. Each partition can belong to a different storage group. The relationship between storage groups, databases, tables, and table spaces is shown in Figure 7.1.

7.4.1   The CREATE TABLESPACE statement

We use the SQL CREATE TABLESPACE statement to explicitly create our own simple or partitioned table spaces. We can issue this statement interactively or it can be embedded within an application. The simplest format of the CREATE TABLESPACE statement is as follows:

```
CREATE TABLESPACE table-space-name
       IN database-name
```

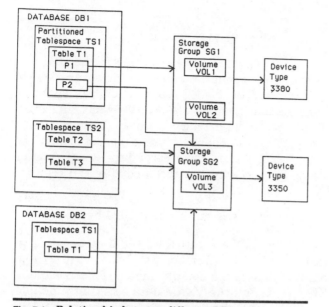

Fig. 7.1   Relationship between different DB2 objects.

Example 7.4   The following creates a table space named TBLSP100 in database DBTST100 and a table space named TBLSP200 in the default database:

```
CREATE TABLESPACE tblsp100
     IN dbtst100

CREATE TABLESPACE tblsp200
```

When we use CREATE TABLESPACE with the keyword IN to create our own table space, DB2 will create our table space in the database we specify and use the default storage for that database. In our example, the default storage group for database DBTST100 is defined as TST100 in the previous section. The database named followed by the keyword IN must be already defined to DB2. If we create our table space without the IN keyword as we did for table space TBLSP200, DB2 will create our table space in the default database DSNDB04 and use the default storage group SYSDEFLT.

The USING clause.   The USING clause allows us to name the storage group in which we want to create our table space if it is other than the default storage group of the database. The USING clause is coded as follows:

```
USING STOGROUP storage-group-name
     PRIQTY integer
     SECQTY integer
```

```
ERASE YES or NO
FREEPAGE integer
PCTFREE integer
```

The storage group we want to use must be defined in the DB2 catalog. DB2 will use this storage group to define the necessary VSAM data sets for our table space. The PRIQTY and SECQTY keywords specify the primary and secondary storage spaces we want DB2 to allocate to the VSAM data sets. The primary storage spaces can be at most 4,194,304 bytes and the secondary storage spaces cannot be greater than 131,068 bytes. The primary or secondary storage spaces are calculated as follows: If n is the integer specified after the keyword PRIQTY or SECQTY,

$$\text{Primary/secondary storage spaces} = n \times 1024 \text{ bytes}$$

The default number for PRIQTY and SECQTY is 3 if we do not specify any PRIQTY or SECQTY. If the number we pick for PRIQTY or SECQTY is less than 3, DB2 uses the default number for those quantities. If we want DB2 to erase all the VSAM data sets that it defines for the table space when the table space is deleted, we use the ERASE YES option. The ERASE NO option will not erase those data sets and is also the default option.

When DB2 acquires storage spaces for the VSAM data sets, it does so by the number of pages. The integer n coded after the FREEPAGE keyword specifies the existence of a free page after every n pages of data when the table is loaded. The integer n can be from 0 to 255; the default number is 0, which means that there are no free pages. We can also leave a percentage of a page as free space by using the keyword PCTFREE with an integer from 0 to 99 specifying the percentage of free space of each page when the table is loaded. DB2 will leave 5 percent of free space in each page as a default.

Example 7.5   Suppose we want to create a table space named TBLSP100 in database DBTST100 using storage group TST200 with the following:

Primary storage space is 24,576 bytes.

Secondary storage space is 8192 bytes.

Erase the VSAM data sets when the table space no longer exists.

Leave a free page after every four pages of data.

Leave 10 percent of each page as free space.

We would do so as follows:

```
CREATE TABLESPACE tblsp100
            IN dbtst100
   USING STOGROUP tst200
      PRIQTY 24
      SECQTY 8
```

```
        ERASE YES
     FREEPAGE 4
        PCTFREE 10
```

The NUMPARTS clause. A partitioned table space can be created with the NUMPARTS clause. When we have a large table, it is better to divide the available space into partitions so that we can manage them easily. To a user all the data in a partitioned table space still belong to a logical table, but physically, the data in each partition can belong to a different storage group. With a partitioned table space, we can load each partition or do table maintenance on each partition independently without affecting the others partitions. The NUMPARTS clause is used as follows:

```
NUMPARTS integer
    ( PART integer USING clause ,
    . . . . . . . . . ,
    . . . . . . . . . ,
    PART integer USING clause )
```

The integer after the keyword NUMPARTS defines the number of partitions for our table space; we can define from 1 to 64 partitions for a single table space. Each partition can be identified in the PART clause and defined with the USING clause. If a partition is not defined with a PART clause, DB2 will first use the USING clause outside the NUMPARTS clause to define it if there is one; otherwise, the default storage group will be used for its definition.

Example 7.6   The following will create a partitioned table space named TBLSP100 in database DBTST100:

```
CREATE TABLESPACE tblsp100
               IN dbtst100
   USING STOGROUP tst200
      PRIQTY 8
      SECQTY 8
      NUMPARTS 4
      ( PART 1 USING STOGROUP tst300
         PRIQTY 8
         SECQTY 8 ,
      PART 2 USING STOGROUP tst400
         PRIQTY 8
         SECQTY 8 )
```

The BUFFERPOOL clause. A table space can have a different buffer pool from the database it is in when it is defined with the BUFFERPOOL clause. The use of the BUFFERPOOL clause for a table space is the same as for a database.

The CLOSE and the DSETPASS clauses.   If we want the VSAM data sets containing the data for our table space to stay open even if the table is not in use, we must use the option CLOSE NO when we create the table space. The default option is CLOSE YES. The keyword DSETPASS followed by a password is used only if there is a password to be used when DB2 accesses the VSAM data sets.

7.4.2   The ALTER TABLESPACE statement

The FREEPAGE, PCTFREE, BUFFERPOOL, CLOSE, DSETPASS, and PART clauses of a table space can be modified with an ALTER TABLESPACE statement. The ALTER TABLESPACE statement can be used in an interactive mode or in an embedded mode as follows:

```
ALTER TABLESPACE database-name.table-space-name
    BUFFERPOOL BP0/BP1/BP2
        CLOSE YES/NO
    DSETPASS password
        PART integer
    FREEPAGE integer
        PCTFREE integer
```

The table space name is qualified with the database name to which it belongs. The default database DSNDB04 is assumed if the database is not specified. The PART clause is used only if we want to alter a partition of a partitioned table space. It is used only to change the FREEPAGE and the PCTFREE of a partition, and we can only change one partition at a time with a single ALTER TABLESPACE statement. One thing we must remember when using the DSETPASS clause is that it only changes the password DB2 uses to access the VSAM data sets. The actual password of the VSAM data sets must be changed through the access method services.

7.4.3   The DROP TABLESPACE statement

If for any reason we want to change a clause for a table space to one that is other than the allowable clauses in the ALTER TABLESPACE statement, we have to delete the table space and redefine it. The DROP TABLESPACE statement deletes a table space. When a table space is dropped, all the tables defined in that table space are also dropped. Its format is:

```
DROP TABLESPACE table-space-name
```

7.5   Defining Your Own Data Sets

Normally, the data sets created by DB2 through the storage groups meet most of our requirements. However, we can also define and manage the VSAM data sets ourselves without using the storage groups. In order to do so, we must use the Access Method Services to create the necessary VSAM data sets for our table space. All the data sets must be defined before we can create our table space. The Access Method Services command used to define a data set is beyond the scope of this book; readers should refer to the IBM Access Method manuals for information about how to create and manage the VSAM data sets. When we create our table space using our own data set, we specify it in the USING clause as follows:

```
USING VCAT vsam-catalog-name
    FREEPAGE integer
    PCTFREE integer
```

The key expression USING VCAT followed by a VSAM catalog name tells DB2 that we are using a data set defined in a VSAM catalog rather than a storage group. FREEPAGE and PCTFREE are the only two options in the USING clause when we are not using a storage group.

Similarly, if we have a partitioned table space, we must define all the necessary data sets for each partition in the NUMPARTS clause before we can define the table space.

Example 7.7   The following will create a table space named TBLSP100 in database DBTST100 in the VSAM catalog named VCAT100:

```
CREATE TABLESPACE tblsp100
                IN dbtst100
    USING VCAT vcat100
        FREEPAGE 4
        PCTFREE 10
```

In order for DB2 to be able to locate the data set we defined for the table space in Example 7.7, the name of the data set must be created as entries in the VSAM catalog in the following format:

```
VCAT100.DSNDBx.DBTST100.TBLSP100.I0001.A001
```

A sample access method command to define a VSAM data set for the table space in Example 7.7 can be as follows:

```
DEFINE CLUSTER
    (NAME(VCAT100.DSNDBC.DBTST100.TBLSP100.I0001.A001)
    TRACKS(45 5)
    VOLUMES(CDP150)
    CONTROLINTERVALSIZE(4096)
    NONINDEXED
    RECORDSIZE(4089 4089)
    REUSE
    SHAREOPTIONS(3 3) )
DATA
    (NAME(VCAT100.DSNDBD.DBTST100.TBLSP100.I0001.A001) )
```

We can see that the catalog, database, and table space names are part of the data set name. If the entry is created for the cluster part of the data set, the second qualifier of the name is coded DSNDBC; otherwise, DSNDBD is coded for the data part of the data set. Again, all the information about the cluster or data part of a VSAM data set can be found in the Access Method Services manuals. Each name must contain the string I0001 and end with a string Annn. A001 means that it is the first data set and A002 is the second data set, etc. When we define our own data sets, we must perform all the functions that are normally handled by DB2 when a storage group is used. If a table space is dropped, we must delete the corresponding data sets. Also, when we delete the data sets, we must delete the table spaces that use those data sets. Likewise, we must define additional data sets when our table expands and more spaces are needed.

7.6   Conclusion

We should like to conclude this chapter with a reminder to our readers that the discussion in this chapter only touches the subject of DB2 objects spaces. There is a lot more to be said about this topic which we believe is not a real concern to an application programmer or a user.

Chapter 8

Advanced DB2 Features

Up to this point, we've been talking primarily about basic sequential retrieval. In this chapter, we'll be talking about some of the advanced features of DB2: the index which allows us to retrieve data from a table in a sequence other than the normal table sequence, the view which allows us to represent data from one or more tables in a different way, and some advanced SQL coding techniques.

8.1 Advanced SQL Coding Techniques

Most of the SQL coding techniques we've learned so far are fairly simple. Although we've learned to use all the clauses in a SELECT statement and all the built-in functions, our normal environment usually requires a fair amount of complexity in processing the data. With this in mind, DB2 provides us with some advanced capabilities to fulfill our processing needs.

8.1.1 The WHENEVER statement

We've seen in Chapter 4 that it is a good programming practice to check the SQL Communication Area (SQLCA) after issuing an SQL statement in an application program. By examining the SQLCA, we can find out if there are any errors during the execution of our SQL statement. With the use of the SQL WHENEVER statement in our application program, we can have the system examine the SQLCA for us and perform the necessary actions when an abnormal condition occurs. Basically, there are three types of the WHENEVER statement for the three possible abnormal conditions:

```
WHENEVER NOT FOUND     CONTINUE
                       or GOTO    label
                       or GO TO   label
```

```
WHENEVER SQLERROR      CONTINUE
                       or GOTO     label
                       or GO TO    label

WHENEVER SQLWARNING    CONTINUE
                       or GOTO     label
                       or GO TO    label
```

The first WHENEVER statement is used when we want the system to perform some actions in a NOT FOUND condition; that is, the SQL return code (SQLCODE) is $+100$. When an error condition occurs in the execution of our SQL statement (i.e., the value of SQLCODE is negative), the second type of WHENEVER statement is used. If we want the system to perform some actions when the SQLCODE is returned with a positive value other than $+100$, we should use the third type of the WHENEVER statement.

Example 8.1   Suppose in our application program we want the program to do the following: continue with the execution if a warning occurs, go to ERROR-HANDLER if an error occurs, and go to NXT-REC if a NOT FOUND condition occurs. The code for this is:

```
ID DIVISION.
...
    ...
ENVIRONMENT DIVISION.
    ...
    ...
DATA DIVISION.
    ...
    ...
WORKING-STORAGE SECTION.
    ...
    ...
    ...
    EXEC SQL INCLUDE SQLCA END-EXEC.
    ...
    ...
PROCEDURE DIVISION.
    ...
    ...
    ...
    EXEC SQL WHENEVER SQLWARNING CONTINUE END-EXEC.
    EXEC SQL WHENEVER SQLERROR    GOTO ERROR-HANDLER END-EXEC.
    EXEC SQL WHENEVER NOT FOUND   GO TO NXT-REC END-EXEC.
    EXEC SQL .....        END-EXEC.
    ...
    ...
    ...
ERROR-HANDLER.
    ...
    ...
    ...
```

```
   . . .
NXT-REC.
   . . .
   . . .
   . . .
   . . .
```

The SQL WHENEVER statement can be coded anywhere in the main body of a PL/1 program. In a Cobol program, it can be anywhere in the PROCEDURE DIVISION. We can have more than one WHENEVER statement of the same type in an application program. In other words, each SQL statement in the program is affected by the most recently preceded WHENEVER statement.

8.1.2 The JOIN technique

The SELECT statement we've seen in Chapters 4 and 5 deals mainly with data residing in one table only. Usually in our daily processing requirement, we need to process data residing in more than one table. In our hospital environment, we want a list of patients who were admitted to the hospital after 1986. The patient name is located in the PATIENT table and the admit date is located in the VISIT table. The only link that exists between the two tables is the patient ID number. We need to select all the patients in our PATIENT table who have one or more entries in the VISIT table and have an admit date later than 1986. The process of selecting data from more than one table and combining them into one result table is a JOIN. The SELECT statement used to build the result table is shown in Example 8.2.

Example 8.2   The following will select all patients who were admitted after 1986:

```
SELECT visit.idno,patient.patname,visit.addate
   FROM visit,patient
 WHERE visit.idno   = patient.patno AND
         visit.addate > '860000'
```

The result table is as follows:

IDNO	PATNAME	ADDATE
0005	jackson	860110
0028	brown	860520
0017	parker	860210
0042	lee	860617

In order to provide us with the above result table, DB2 would have to parse our request into two SELECT statements. The first SELECT statement would retrieve all IDNO in the VISIT table with an admit date greater than 1986. The second SELECT statement would retrieve all patient names in the PATIENT table with PATNO equal to the IDNO from the first SELECT statement. The result table is the combination of the results of the two SELECT statements. Joining does not require us to use more than one table or impose a limit on the number of tables we can join together. In fact, it is absolutely valid to join a table to itself.

When specifying the column names in a JOIN, if a column name is the same in more than one table, we must qualify it with the table name to tell DB2 which table that column is from. In our example, we do not have to qualify the patient ID column because it is called PATNO in the PATIENT table and IDNO in the VISIT table. For documentation purposes, we should always try to qualify the column names in a SELECT statement. Notice that the WHERE clause in the SELECT statement is used to limit the number of rows in the result table to only the ones that satisfy the selection criteria. If we did not have the WHERE clause in the SELECT statement in Example 8.2, the result table would have 72 rows. DB2 would have selected all nine rows in the VISIT table, combined each one of them with all eight rows selected from the PATIENT table and the result table would be totally wrong. Thus when we select data from more than one table, we should try to establish all the search conditions to achieve the correct result. Actually, there is no limit to the number of tables we can join together; however, it becomes impractical when we try to join more than seven tables at one time.

JOIN in an application program. The JOIN technique is perfectly valid when it is used within an application program. If JOIN is used to retrieve data, the SELECT statement must be part of a DECLARE CURSOR statement, since the result table is normally returned with more than one row.

JOIN in an INSERT statement. We've seen in Chapter 5 that we can use a SELECT statement embedded in an INSERT statement to load a table or do a mass insert. If the table to be loaded or inserted requires data from more than one table, we can use the JOIN technique to select data from multiple tables and insert them into the target table.

Example 8.3 Suppose we have a table named PATADM which contains IDNO, PATNAME, BIRTHDATE, SEX, and ADDATE > '860000'. We know that the data we need reside in two different tables: PATIENT and VISIT. The following INSERT statement shows how to join the two tables together and select data for insertion:

```
INSERT INTO patadm
   (idno,patname,birthdate,sex,addate)
SELECT idno,patname,birthdate, sex,addate
   FROM patient, visit
   WHERE visit.idno   = patient.patno  AND
       visit.addate > '860000'
```

8.1.3   The UNION operator

The UNION operator is used to combine the result of two or more SE-
LECT statements into a single result table. The UNION operator is
used as follows:

```
SELECT statement . . . UNION or UNION ALL
. . .                  UNION or UNION ALL
. . .                  UNION or UNION ALL
SELECT statement . . .
```

When DB2 builds the combined result table, it eliminates all the
duplicates. However, if the keyword ALL is used in the UNION operation, DB2 will keep all the duplicates.

Example 8.4   Suppose we want to have a list of the IDs of all the patients who
were born after 1960 or who were admitted to the hospital after 1986. There is
no relationship between a patient's birth date and his or her admit date. The
combined result table can be obtained with the following statement:

```
SELECT patient.patno
   FROM patient
 WHERE patient.birthdate > '600000'
     UNION
 SELECT visit.idno
   FROM visit
 WHERE visit.addate > '860000'
```

The result of the first SELECT statement is a temporary table with two rows:

PATNO
0028
0017

The result of the second SELECT statement is a temporary table with four rows:

IDNO
0005
0028
0017
0042

The combined result contains only four rows because DB2 eliminates all the duplicates:

0028
0017
0005
0042

If we had coded UNION ALL in Example 8.4, the combined result table would contain six rows because all the duplicates are kept. Since DB2 combines the result of each SELECT statement into a single table, the columns specified in each SELECT statement must have the same data type and length and each SELECT statement must specify the same number of columns. The combined result table can be sorted by using the ORDER BY clause after the last SELECT statement in the operation as follows:

```
SELECT statement ...   UNION or UNION ALL
...               UNION or UNION ALL
...               UNION or UNION ALL
SELECT statement ...
ORDER BY integer
```

Each SELECT statement used with the UNION operator must not contain an ORDER BY clause. Since the columns in the combined result table contain values from multiple SELECT statements, they do not have any name. We must use an integer in the ORDER BY clause to specify the column we want the table to be ordered by. The integer must correspond to the position of the column in the result table.

Example 8.5   The SELECT statements in Example 8.4 can be coded as follows to yield a collated combined result table on patient Id number:

```
SELECT patient.patno
   FROM patient
  WHERE patient.birthdate > '600000'
     UNION
  SELECT visit.idno
     FROM visit
  WHERE visit.addate > '860000'
  ORDER BY 1
```

The SELECT statement embedded in an INSERT statement to load a table or do a mass insert cannot contain the UNION operator.

UNION operator in an application program.   The SELECT statements used with the UNION operator must be part of a DECLARE CURSOR statement when they are used within an application program. The UNION operator also cannot be used in a DECLARE CURSOR statement if it contains the FOR UPDATE OF clause. In other words, the UNION operator is used in retrieval mode only.

8.1.4   The subquery

The SQL coding techniques we've seen so far deal only with one level of query. One of the advanced features of DB2 is that it allows us to nest one SELECT statement within another to perform complex search criteria. There is practically no limit to the number of SELECT statements we can nest together. However, for performance reasons, nesting more than five levels of subqueries is not recommended. Nesting the SELECT statements can be done by using either the WHERE or the HAVING clause. The SELECT statement contained in a WHERE or a HAVING clause is called a "subquery," and the SELECT statement that contains it is called the "outer-level" SELECT. At each level of subquery, we can use the boolean operators AND or OR to connect multiple subqueries together. The table referred to in the subquery can be the same as or different from the table used in the outer-level SELECT statement. The format of a SELECT statement with a subquery is as follows:

```
SELECT . . .
    FROM . . .
    WHERE . . . ( SELECT . . .
                    FROM . . .
                    WHERE . . . )
```

or

```
SELECT . . .
    FROM . . .
    WHERE . . .
 GROUP BY . . .
    HAVING . . . ( SELECT . . .
                    FROM . . .
                    WHERE . . . )
```

Formats of subqueries.   Whether we use the WHERE or the HAVING clause to embed our subquery, we must use one of the four formats depending on how we want to build our search criteria. Each format has a different meaning and will yield a different result. When DB2 encounters a SELECT statement with an embedded subquery, it will perform the subquery first; the result of the subquery is then placed in the WHERE or HAVING clause of the outer-level SELECT to build the search condition.

In the first format, the subquery is placed right after the comparison operator. When using this format, the result of the subquery must yield a table that has one column and only one row or value.

Example 8.6   The following will obtain a list of all the physicians in the PHYSICIAN table who earn more than the average salary:

```
SELECT phyname,phyno,department,salary
    FROM physician
```

```
WHERE salary  > ( SELECT AVG(salary)
                  FROM physician )
```

When DB2 evaluates the subquery, it returns one single value, which is the average salary ($59,684.57) of all the physicians in the PHYSICIAN table. That figure is then placed after the comparison operator. The result table is as follows:

PHYNAME	PHYNO	DEPARTMENT	SALARY
thompson	432	neurology	76540
burton	479	cardiology	85786

In the second format, the subquery is placed after the keyword ALL or ANY following the comparison operator. The result of the subquery using in this format will return a table with one column of zero or more rows.

Example 8.7   The following will produce a list of all the physicians who earn more than any physician in the department of general medicine:

```
SELECT phyname,phyno,department,salary
   FROM physician
 WHERE salary  > ALL
       (SELECT salary
        FROM physician
      WHERE department = 'general medicine   ' OR
            department = 'dermatology        ')
```

The subquery in Example 8.7 returns three values: 43,720, 43,658, and 59,670. In order to satisfy the condition of the WHERE clause in the outer-level SELECT statement, the salary selected must be greater than the largest value in the subquery (i.e., 59,670). The ALL keyword really means "all the values returned by the subquery." The result table is as follows:

PHYNAME	PHYNO	DEPARTMENT	SALARY
thompson	432	neurology	76540
burton	479	cardiology	85786

Similarly the keyword ANY means "any of the values returned by the subquery."

We've seen in Chapter 4 how to use the keyword IN in the WHERE clause to specify that the value in an expression must belong to a set of values. But in the third format, the keyword IN is used to specify that the value in an expression must belong to the set of values returned by the subquery.

Example 8.8   The following will list all the patients who were admitted after 1986:

```
SELECT patient.patno,patient.patname
   FROM patient
 WHERE patno    IN
       ( SELECT idno
         FROM visit
         WHERE addate > '860000')
```

The result table is as follows: -

PATNO	PATNAME	ADDATE
0005	jackson	860110
0028	brown	860520
0017	parker	860210
0042	lee	860617

The fourth format is used to specify a condition to retrieve data depending on the existence of the values returned by the subquery. The keyword EXISTS or NOT EXISTS is used after the WHERE clause in the outer-level SELECT statement and is followed by the subquery. The keyword EXISTS is used when we want DB2 to retrieve data from the outer-level SELECT statement only if at least one row is returned from the subquery. On the other hand, the keyword NOT EXISTS specifies that data are selected from the outer-level SELECT statement only if no row is returned from the subquery.

Example 8.9   The following will count the number of patient visits to each physician if the VISIT table is not empty:

```
SELECT mdno, COUNT(*)
  FROM TEST.VISIT
  GROUP BY mdno
    HAVING EXISTS
      ( SELECT *
          FROM visit )
```

The result table is:

MDNO	COUNT(*)
234	2
612	1
345	2
867	1
432	1
479	1
916	1

Since we are only concerned with the existence of the values in the subquery but not the values themselves, we do not have to specify any column name in the subquery. The asterisk (*) can be used in the subquery as in Example 8.9. We must keep in mind that the UNION operator and the ORDER BY clause can be used in the outer-level SELECT statement but not in the subquery. The SELECT statement that is part of an INSERT statement can also contain subqueries. We can have an INSERT statement as follows:

```
INSERT INTO table.name
  ( column.name, ..., ..., column.name )
  SELECT ...
     FROM ...
   WHERE ... ( SELECT ...
               FROM ...
               WHERE ... )
```

Subqueries in an application program. If a SELECT statement with subqueries is embedded in an application program and is used for data retrieval, the outer-level SELECT statement must be part of a DE-CLARE CURSOR statement.

Subqueries in UPDATE and DELETE statements. The outer-level statement of a subquery can also be an UPDATE statement or a DELETE statement. The subquery used in these statement is part of the WHERE clause. We must make sure that the table referred to by the subquery is not the same as the table used by the outer-level UP-DATE or DELETE statement. The format of the UPDATE statement and the DELETE statement can be as follows:

```
UPDATE table-name
  SET column-name = expression ,
      ...       = ...          ,
    column-name = expression
  WHERE ... ( SELECT ...
              FROM   ...
              WHERE  ... )

DELETE table-name
  WHERE ... ( SELECT ...
              FROM   ...
              WHERE  ... )
```

Correlated subqueries. Suppose we want to list all the physicians who earn more than the average salary in their department. To do this, for each physician we retrieve, we have to calculate the average salary for his or her department and then compare it with his or her salary before selecting the record. We need a way to tell DB2 to perform that calculation for us for each row it retrieves and that's exactly the function of a "correlated subquery." In the subquery SQL statements we've seen so far, the value or values returned by the subquery do not change based on each row selected because the subquery is only executed once. In an SQL statement using a correlated subquery, DB2 reevaluates the subquery every time it retrieves a new row in the outer-level SQL statement. The general format of a SELECT statement using correlated subquery is as follows:

```
SELECT column-name, ..., column-name
  FROM table-name correlation-name,
     ...         ,
     table-name
WHERE column-name >
          ( SELECT ...
             FROM table-name
             WHERE column-name = correlation-name.column-name)
```

Example 8.10 The following will select all the physicians who earn more than the average salary of their department:

```
SELECT phyname,phyno,department,salary
  FROM TEST.VISIT hisdept
WHERE salary >  ( SELECT AVG(salary)
                    FROM TEST.VISIT
                    WHERE department = hisdept.department )
```

To code a correlated subquery, we must assign a correlation name which specifies the current row of the outer-level SQL statement. The correlation name must follow the table name associated with it and be preceded by a space. In the subquery, we qualify the column name with the correlation name to tell DB2 that the value of that column is from the outer-level SQL statement. A correlation name can be a character string containing from 1 to 18 characters and must not be any of the SQL reserved words. In Example 8.10, when DB2 encounters HISDEPT in the outer-level FROM clause, it knows that we're using a correlated subquery because HISDEPT is not preceded by the comma that is used to separate table names. In a correlated subquery, DB2 evaluates the outer-level statement first, substitutes all the column names in the subquery that are qualified by the correlation name with their current value, and then evaluates the subquery. It does that for every row it retrieves from the table in the outer-level SQL statement. For the purpose of our discussion, suppose our PHYSICIAN table looks like this:

PHYNAME	PHYNO	DEPARTMENT	HIREDATE	SALARY
stern	345	general medicine	750312	43720
mitchum	867	obstetrics	661211	58760
hoffman	860	obstetrics	661201	60850
miller	234	dermatology	670423	59670

PHYNAME	PHYNO	DEPARTMENT	HIREDATE	SALARY
green	230	dermatology	680515	61240
thompson	432	neurology	760322	76540
cooper	415	neurology	750120	74420
burton	479	cardiology	470506	85786
francis	482	cardiology	600830	80550
jones	916	pediatrics	731205	49658
stein	612	general medicine	801115	43658

Example 8.10 would return the following result:

PHYNAME	PHYNO	DEPARTMENT	SALARY
stern	345	general medicine	43720
hoffman	860	obstetrics	60850
green	230	dermatology	61240
thompson	432	neurology	76540
burton	479	cardiology	85786

Like a regular subquery, a correlated subquery can also be used with the HAVING clause. The JOIN operation is also allowable in the outer-level statement of a correlated subquery. Correlated subqueries can also be used in an INSERT, UPDATE, and DELETE statement. Correlated subqueries used in these statements follow the same rules as the regular subqueries. SQL statements embedded within an application program can also use correlated subqueries, and they must follow the same rules as the regular subqueries.

Example 8.11   Suppose we only keep the patients' records for 10 years. After deleting all the rows in the PATIENT table that are more than 10 years old, we need also to delete all the rows associated with those patients' records in the VISIT table. In other words we want to delete all the rows in the VISIT table that do not have any corresponding patient record in the PATIENT table. We could do so as follows:

```
DELETE FROM visit thisrec
    WHERE NOT EXISTS
        ( SELECT *
            FROM test.patient
                WHERE patno = thisrec.idno )
```

8.2 Index

Suppose in our hospital we have a list which contains information about all the patients such as our PATIENT table. When patients are admitted to the hospital we want to locate their medical records using their ID numbers. To do that we would have to look at each patient's ID number, starting from the top of our patient list, until we find a matching ID number. However, it would make the admitting clerk's job much easier if our patient list is ordered by patient ID number. That's exactly the result of a DB2 index; it makes it look as though we have another list with all the records ordered by an index key, in our case the patient ID number. With an index by patient ID number, given an ID number, we can avoid a sequential search and go directly to the record we want.

8.2.1 What is a DB2 index?

A DB2 index is basically a set of pointers that point to the values of data in one or more columns of a table being indexed. Each table can have more than one index and each index is separate and has its own index space. Indexes are VSAM Entry-Sequenced Data Sets (ESDS) that hold pointers to the values of data in a table. Each index can have from 1 to 64 ESDSs, and it belongs to the same database as the table. Each index is built and maintained by DB2 after it has been defined to DB2. Every time a table is updated, DB2 will automatically update each index of the table to reflect the changes. A DB2 index allows us to access the data in a more efficient way and its existence is totally transparent to the users and applications. Since DB2 is a nonprocedural language, we do not tell DB2 to use an index to access the data in our SQL statements. In fact, DB2 will only use an index to get to the data when executing our SQL statement if it finds that more efficient.

8.2.2 The CREATE INDEX statement

The SQL CREATE INDEX is used to create an index of a DB2 table. This statement can be used interactively or can be embedded in an application program. Like a DB2 table, an index needs some storage space to store its pointers. The CREATE INDEX statement also creates an index space in the database of the table being indexed. A simple general format of the CREATE INDEX statement is as follows:

```
CREATE (UNIQUE) INDEX index-name ON table-name
    ( column-name     ASC/DESC   ,
      ...             ...        ,
      column-name     ASC/DESC   )
```

The keyword UNIQUE is used only if a unique index is to be created. In a unique index, no rows can have the same value for the index key. If our PATIENT table contains a unique index of patient IDs,

DB2 will not allow us to assign the same ID number to two different patients. Each index defined to DB2 must possess a unique name. The naming convention for an index is the same as for a table name. Except when we define our own data sets for the index, the index name must be at most eight characters long. The table to be indexed is named after the keyword ON and the table must already be defined to DB2. The table may or may not contain data. One or more columns that make up the index key are enclosed in a pair of parentheses and separated by a comma. If a column is to be ordered in descending sequence, we must specify the keyword DESC after the column name; otherwise the default sequence is ascending (ASC). The maximum number of columns an index can contain is 16.

Example 8.12 The following will create a unique index by patient ID that is named PATXID NO and a nonunique index by patient name and sex that is named PATXNAME for the PATIENT table:

```
CREATE UNIQUE INDEX patxidno ON patient
      ( patno     ASC       )

   CREATE INDEX patxname ON patient
      ( patname ASC,
        sex        ASC       )
```

When we create the PATXID NO index, if our table already contains data and there are two patients with the same ID number, an error occurs and DB2 will not create the index. As for the PATXNAME index, since it is nonunique, more than one patient with the same name and sex may exist. In other words more than one row with the same index key is acceptable.

The USING clause.   Since each index is separate and must have its own index space, we need to specify the storage devices through which the physical spaces of each index space can be met. Like a table space, the USING clause can be used in a CREATE INDEX statement to specify the storage group in which the index space will belong or the VSAM data sets that we create for the index space. If we decide to manage the VSAM data sets (rather than let DB2 manage them), we must define them prior to creating the index. If we do not use the USING clause, DB2 will create the index space in the default storage group of the database. In fact, the syntax of the USING clause in a CREATE INDEX statement is exactly the same as in a CREATE TABLESPACE statement.

Example 8.13 Suppose we want to create a unique index by Patient ID named PATXID NO using storage group TST200 with the following:

Primary storage space 20,480 bytes
Secondary storage space 8192 bytes

Erase the VSAM data sets when the table space no longer exists

Leave a free page after every five pages of data

Leave 15 percent of each page as free space

The code to do so is:

```
CREATE UNIQUE INDEX patxidno ON patient
        ( patno          ASC          )
    USING STOGROUP tst200
        PRIQTY 20
        SECQTY 8
          ERASE YES
      FREEPAGE 5
      PCTFREE 15
```

Example 8.14 The following will create a unique index by Patient ID that is named PATXID NO using the data set we define in the VSAM catalog named VCAT100:

```
CREATE UNIQUE INDEX patxidno ON patient
          ( patno          ASC          )
        USING VCAT vcat100
          FREEPAGE 4
            PCTFREE 10
```

The CLUSTER clause. When a table is loaded, the rows are stored in the order that they come in but not necessarily in the order of any index. However, we can specify one and only one index in each table to be a cluster index, in which case DB2 will try to store the rows as close as possible in the order of their index key value when the table is loaded. Although it is totally transparent to the user or application whether a cluster index exists or not, it is significantly more efficient to access data through a cluster index than through a noncluster index. The CLUSTER clause is used to define a cluster index. Like a table space, we can also define a partitioned index for a partitioned table space as follows; in this case it must also be a cluster index:

```
CLUSTER
   ( PART integer VALUES ( constant ,
                          ...      ,
                          constant ) USING clause ,
   ...     ...     ...    ( ...     ,
                          ...      ,
                          ...) ...
      PART integer VALUES   ( constant ,
                          ...      ,
                          constant ) USING clause )
```

The PART keyword is used to specify each partition in a partitioned index. The number of partitions in a partitioned index must match the number of partitions defined in the NUMPARTS clause of the partitioned table space. We specify the highest key value, if the key column is in ascending order (the lowest key value if the key column is in descending order), of each partition after the keyword VALUES. If the index key is made up of more than one column, the highest or lowest key values of the key columns are specified in the order in which they are defined in the index key.

Example 8.15   The following will create a unique cluster index by Patient ID that is named PATXID NO:

```
CREATE UNIQUE INDEX patxidno ON patient
      (patno      ASC      )
    CLUSTER
```

Example 8.16   This will create a partitioned index by patient name and sex that is named PATXNAME:

```
PATXNAME.
CREATE INDEX patxname ON patient
        ( patname ASC,
          sex        ASC        )
    CLUSTER
        ( PART    1    VALUES ( 'E', 'M') ,
          PART    2    VALUES ( 'J', 'M') ,
          PART    3    VALUES ( 'O', 'M') ,
          PART    4    VALUES ( 'T', 'M') ,
          PART    5    VALUES ( '9', 'M') )
```

In Example 8.16, the index key values are assigned to five parts. Partition 1 contains all the patient names from the letter A to the letter E, either male of female. The letter M is used for the highest value in the SEX column because its value can be either F or M, and M comes after F in the alphabet. The number 9 specified in partition 5 means that any names that do not fit in partition 4 will be in partition 5. Remember that we can only have one cluster index for each table. As with a partition in a partitioned table space, we can define each partition in a partitioned index in a different storage group, or we can manage the data sets for each partition ourselves with the USING clause. If we plan to manage the data sets ourselves, we must use the access method services to define the data sets for each part before creating the index.

The BUFFERPOOL clause.   A different buffer pool can be specified for an index if the BUFFERPOOL clause is used. If the BUFFERPOOL clause is omitted, the index will have the same buffer pool as the database it is in. The use of the BUFFERPOOL clause for an index is the same as for a database.

The CLOSE and the DSETPASS clauses. The use of the CLOSE and DSETPASS clauses for an index is the same as for a table space.

Example 8.17 Suppose we want to create a unique index by Patient ID that is named PATXID NO using the storage group TST200. When the index is deleted, the data sets will not be erased. Use buffer pool BP1, close the data sets when the index is not in use, and use the password SECRET to access the data sets. The code is as follows:

```
CREATE UNIQUE INDEX patxidno ON patient
        ( patno    ASC    )
    USING STOGROUP tst200
        ERASE  no
  BUFFERPOOL  bp1
       CLOSE  yes
    DSETPASS  secret
```

Since an index is maintained by DB2 after it's been defined, we should consider minimizing the number of indexes defined in the columns that are frequently updated because DB2 has to update each index every time a change is made to those columns.

8.2.3 The ALTER INDEX statement

Once an index has been defined, we can only modify the BUFFER-POOL, CLOSE, DSETPASS, PART, FREEPAGE, and PCTFREE clauses. Like other ALTER statements, it can be used interactively or can be embedded in an application program. The rules regarding the use of the keywords within an ALTER INDEX statement are the same as for an ALTER TABLESPACE statement. Its format is:

```
ALTER INDEX  index-name
 BUFFERPOOL  BP0/BP1/BP2
      CLOSE  YES/NO
   DSETPASS  password
       PART  integer
   FREEPAGE  integer
    PCTFREE  integer
```

8.2.4 The DROP INDEX statement

The DROP INDEX statement is used to drop an unpartitioned index. A partitioned index can only be dropped when we drop the table space associated with it. The statement is used as follows:

```
DROP INDEX index-name
```

When we delete an index, all its definitions in the DB2 catalog are also deleted and DB2 will not make use of it to access the associated table. Suppose we have an index A defined on table T and an application program that uses index A to access table T. For some reason, we have to drop index A and redefine it. We've seen in Chapter 3 that before an application program can be executed, we must go through a process called "binding" to link it to the DB2 tables it accesses. If the application program is executed after index A is deleted and before it is recreated, DB2 will automatically rebind the program for us and will not make use of the old index. However, when the program is executed again after index A is recreated, the program will not make use of the new index unless we rebind the program ourselves.

8.3   View

We will go back to the list we have in our hospital which contains information about all the patients such as in our PATIENT table. The Patient Relation department in our hospital requests a complete patient list so that it can send out a patient questionnaire. Some of the information on the patient list is confidential; we only want to release the patient name and address information to the Patient Relation department. What we have to do is to send the whole patient list to the Patient Relation department after masking out all the confidential information on that list. Thus a view can be thought of as a window through which we can look at a selected portion our data.

8.3.1   What is a view?

View refers to a group of columns that a specific group of users or application programs may access. No single table can contain all the information needed for every application and also certain kinds of information need to have limited access (i.e., salary, etc.). Therefore, a view can be created to contain selected columns and rows from one or more tables. Although there are some restrictions on the types of operations that can be done on a view, to a user a view looks exactly like a table. The main difference between a table and a view is that a view does not require any storage spaces to hold its data and we cannot create an index of it. A view uses the data from the tables on which it is based. Like other DB2 objects, the definition of a view is stored in the DB2 catalog after it is created. Because a view uses the data from its base table or tables, all the changes made to the data in the base table or tables are reflected in it. If a base table possesses an index, DB2 will make use of it to improve performance when data are accessed through a view. A view can be created by anyone once he or she has the authorization. Once a view is defined, we can retrieve data from it just as we do from a table.

8.3.2 The CREATE VIEW statement

The SQL CREATE VIEW is used to create a view of one or more DB2 tables. The statement can be used interactively or can be embedded in an application program. The general format of the CREATE VIEW statement is as follows:

```
CREATE VIEW view-name
        ( column-name ,
          ...
          column-name  )
   AS SELECT statement ...
   WITH CHECK OPTION
```

Each name given to a view must be unique and cannot be the same as any existing tables in the DB2 catalog. The names assigned to DB2 views follow the same rules as the names assigned to DB2 tables. Like a DB2 table, we can assign a unique name to each column in a view. The name we assign to a column in a view can be the same as it is in the result table, or if we omit the column names from a view, DB2 will use the names of the columns in the result table as column names for the view. The view definition is in the DB2 catalog. Every time DB2 encounters an SQL statement that uses a view, it processes the view definition in the catalog and builds a table for that view.

The SELECT statement is used after the keyword AS to select the column or columns of one or more tables from which the view will be created. The SELECT statement used in a CREATE VIEW statement is exactly the same as a SELECT statement used to retrieve data from one or more DB2 tables except that the clauses ORDER BY and FOR UPDATE OF cannot be used in a SELECT statement when it is used to define a view. The UNION operator cannot be used in a SELECT statement to create a view. The SELECT statement used to define a view can also contain subqueries and correlated subqueries.

Example 8.18   The following will create a view from the PATIENT table that is named PATVADR and contains the patient name, ID number, and address:

```
CREATE VIEW patvadr
   ( patname,patno,address )
  AS SELECT patname,patno,address
     FROM patient
```

As the result of the SELECT statement, the view PATVADR would contain the following information:

PATNAME	PATNO	ADDRESS
smith	0001	123 first street
doe	0010	225 wilshire boulevard
jackson	0005	654 soto street

PATNAME	PATNO	ADDRESS
adams	0003	5674 sunset street
brown	0028	12 willow street
johnson	0020	9534 valley boulevard
parker	0017	7655 grand avenue
lee	0042	7462 santa monica boulevard

Example 8.19   To create a view named PATVINFO from the PATIENT, VISIT, and PHYSICIAN tables which contain patient name, ID number, admit date, discharge date, and physician name, use the following:

```
CREATE VIEW patvinfo
    ( idno,patname,addate,dsdate,phyname )
  AS SELECT idno,patname,addate,dsdate,phyname
    FROM visit,patient,physician
  WHERE visit.idno = patient.patno
    AND visit.mdno = physician.phyno
```

The result of the SELECT statement in the CREATE VIEW statement in Example 8.19 is as follows:

IDNO	PATNAME	ADDATE	DSDATE	PHYNAME
0001	smith	850810	850810	miller
0001	smith	851020	851020	stein
0010	doe	851112	851112	stern
0005	jackson	860110	860110	mitchum
0003	adams	850320	850325	thompson
0028	brown	860520	860520	miller
0020	johnson	851010	851020	burton
0017	parker	860210	860210	jones
0042	lee	860617	860617	stern

Example 8.18 shows an example of a view created on a single table. A view like the one in Example 8.19 is created by using the JOIN operation to combine data from more than one table.

The WITH CHECK OPTION clause.   Although a view does not contain any data, it can be used as though it were a table. Depending on how we define it, a view can be read-only or updatable. With a read-only view, we can only select data from it. A view's data can be updated, deleted, or inserted if the view is updatable. Read-only and updatable views will be discussed in the next section. The WITH CHECK OPTION clause is used only in an updatable view to specify that all inserts and updates to the base table via a view will be rejected if they do not conform to the view definition. If this clause is not used, all inserts and updates will not be validated against the view definition.

8.3.3 Rules regarding views

Since a view can be used as though it were a table, we can use the SQL COMMENT ON statement to add comments to or replace comments from a view exactly as for a table. The format is:

```
COMMENT ON TABLE view-name
    IS text-string
```

or

```
COMMENT ON COLUMN view-name.column-name
    IS text-string
```

or

```
COMMENT ON view-name
    ( column-name IS text-string,
    ...              ...          ,
    column-name IS text-string )
```

We can also create a synonym for a view with the SQL CREATE SYNONYM statement as follows:

```
CREATE SYNONYM synonym
    FOR view-name
```

When we process DB2 data via a view, we must keep in mind that there are certain restrictions on the types of operations we can use, especially in an update mode. Since a view contains a subset of table data, any changes of data through a view will affect the base table and vice versa. As we mentioned in the previous section, a view can be read-only or updatable. A view is updatable only if its definition is based on a single table. A view is read-only if its definition is based on a combination of two or more tables as a result of a JOIN operation. It is also read-only if it is defined by joining a table with itself or if its definition contains any of the built-in functions (AVG, MAX, MIN, etc.) or the keyword DISTINCT or the clauses GROUP BY or HAVING.

If a view definition contains an arithmetic expression (i.e., SALARY * .15), we can retrieve and delete rows from the view, we can update any columns that do not have any arithmetic expression, but we cannot insert any rows in the view. If the base is defined with a column that does not have a default value and that column is not included in the view definition, we can do any operation except inserting rows in the view. Otherwise inserting a row in a view is like inserting a row into a table; we must provide all the values for the columns that do not have a default value and DB2 will assign default values to all the columns in the base table that are not in the view.

8.3.4 The DROP VIEW statement

A view, once it is defined, cannot be altered. We must delete a view and redefine it if we want to make changes to its definition. The SQL statement used to delete a view is as follows:

```
DROP VIEW view-name
```

If the base table is dropped, all the views associated with it will be dropped automatically and all the applications that use those views will also be invalidated. If a view contains all the columns in a base table, any new rows that are added to the base table as result of an ALTER TABLE statement will not show up in the view unless we delete it and redefine it.

Dynamic SQL

Most of the SQL statements we've seen so far can be executed inter-actively or can be embedded within a batch program. Usually, each application program that contains SQL statements performs a single and separate function. For example, we may have one program to up-date the PATIENT table and another one to select data from it, etc. When we code those application programs, we know ahead of time the types of SQL statements we will be using and the types of data we will be updating or getting. Those types of applications use what is called "static" SQL. With static SQL, SQL statements are specified at coding time and the precompiling and binding processes are done during the program preparation stage. However, there is another method which gives our application program greater flexibility and functionality by allowing it to accept SQL statements at run time and execute them dynamically. That method is called "dynamic" SQL. In this chapter, we will discuss the dynamic SQL and how to use it in our application program.

9.1 What Is Dynamic SQL?

Executing SQL statements dynamically in an application program is very similar to issuing SQL statements interactively. When we issue an SQL statement interactively, DB2 has to perform the parsing and binding on the fly before any result can be brought back to us. Simi-larly in an application program using dynamic SQL, each SQL state-ment is input into the application program in the form of a character string at run time. Each SQL statement is then parsed and processed. But DB2 cannot execute those statements immediately; it has to per-form all the precompiling and binding before it can execute them dy-namically. Application programs using dynamic SQL are usually written in PL/1, Assembler, Cobol, or Fortran.

9.2   Executing Non-SELECT Statements Dynamically

When we use dynamic SQL in our application program, if we are certain that our program is a non-SELECT type of program (i.e., only DELETE, INSERT, and UPDATE statements but no SELECT statements will be executed dynamically), we can really simplify the coding. However, if SELECT statements will be issued dynamically in our program, we will have to code our program differently. We will look at the non-SELECT type of programs first and then the SELECT type later.

9.2.1   The EXECUTE IMMEDIATE statement

The EXECUTE IMMEDIATE statement is used only in an application program using dynamic SQL in which no SELECT statements will be issued. As we know, when an SQL statement is executed dynamically, it is brought into the application program at run time as a value of a character string. However, certain SQL statements cannot be executed dynamically, which means that those statements cannot be in the form of a character string but must be hard coded in the application program. With the EXECUTE IMMEDIATE statement, we cannot execute the following statements dynamically: CLOSE, DECLARE, DESCRIBE, EXECUTE, FETCH, INCLUDE, OPEN, PREPARE, SELECT, and WHENEVER. The general format of the EXECUTE IMMEDIATE statement is as follows:

```
EXECUTE IMMEDIATE string-expression or host-variable
```

The SQL statement to be executed dynamically can be a string constant enclosed in quotes or contained in a host variable. If the program is written in Cobol, the host variable containing the SQL statement must be defined as a varying-length string. On the other hand, if the program is written in PL/1, the host variable can be defined as a fixed- or varying-length string.

When DB2 encounters an EXECUTE IMMEDIATE statement, it will try to precompile, bind, and execute the SQL statement specified as its parameter. Normally, before we issue the EXECUTE IMMEDIATE statement in our application program, we should validate the SQL statement in the input buffer to make sure that it can be executed dynamically. After the EXECUTE IMMEDIATE statement is executed, as in static SQL, we must check the SQL Communication Area (SQLCA) to see if the statement has executed successfully. Figure 9.1 shows a sample Cobol program using dynamic SQL. This program does not include any validation routine to check to see if the in-

```
000010   ID DIVISION.
000020   PROGRAM-ID.  SAMPLE4
000030   AUTHOR.   VIET G. TRAN.
000040   DATE-COMPILED.
000050   REMARKS.   THIS PROGRAM READS AN INPUT FILE CONTAINING NON-
000060            SELECT STATEMENTS AND EXECUTES THEM DYNAMICALLY.   EACH
000070            SQL STATEMENT IS CONTAINED IN ONE RECORD AND DELIMITED
000080            BY A SEMI-COLON (;).
000090
000100   ENVIRONMENT DIVISION.
000110
000120   CONFIGURATION SECTION.
000130   SOURCE-COMPUTER.   IBM-3090.
000140   OBJECT-COMPUTER.   IBM-3090.
000150   SPECIAL-NAMES.   C01 IS NEW-PAGE.
000160   INPUT-OUTPUT SECTION.
000170   FILE-CONTROL.
000180
000190       SELECT STMTFILE
000200            ASSIGN TO UT-S-STMTFILE.
000210
000220       SELECT OUTFILE
000230            ASSIGN TO UT-S-OUTFILE.
000240
000250   DATA DIVISION.
000260
000270   FILE SECTION.
000280
000290   FD   STMTFILE
000300        LABEL RECORDS ARE STANDARD
000310        BLOCK CONTAINS 20 RECORDS
000320        RECORDING MODE IS F
000330        RECORD CONTAINS 160 CHARACTERS
000340        DATA RECORD IS STMT-REC.
000350
000360   01   STMT-REC                  PIC X(160).
000370
000380   FD   OUTFILE
000390        LABEL RECORDS ARE OMITTED
000400        BLOCK CONTAINS 0 RECORDS
000410        RECORDING MODE IS F
000420        RECORD CONTAINS 133 CHARACTERS
000430        DATA RECORD IS OUT-REC.
000440
000450   01   OUT-REC.
000460        05   OUT-CCTL             PIC X.
000470        05   OUT-PRT              PIC X(132).
000480
000490   WORKING-STORAGE SECTION.
000500
000510   01   WS-STMT-REC.
000520        05   STMT-BUFFER              PIC X(160) VALUE SPACES.
000530        05   STMT-PART REDEFINES STMT-BUFFER.
000540             10   FIELD1              PIC X(80).
000550             10   FIELD2              PIC X(80).
000560
000570
000580   01   STMT-AREA.
000590        49   STMTL                    PIC S9(4)   COMP.
000600        49   STMTD                    PIC X(160) VALUE SPACES.
```

Fig. 9.1   Sample dynamic SQL program.

```
000610
000620   01   WORK-FIELDS.
000630        05   INREC                    PIC 9(3) VALUE 0.
000640        05   OUTREC                   PIC 9(3) VALUE 0.
000650
000660   01   STATUS-SWITCHES.
000670        05   EOF-SWITCH               PIC X VALUE '0'.
000680             88   EOF                 VALUE '1'.
000690   01   INTERNAL-COUNTS.
000700        05   LYNES                    PIC 9(2) COMP-3 VALUE 99.
000710
000720   01   DETAIL1.
000730        05   FILLER                   PIC X(5)  VALUE SPACES.
000740        05   MSSG                     PIC X(30).
000750        05   FILLER                   PIC X(1)  VALUE SPACE.
000760        05   CODE                     PIC Z(8)9-.
000770        05   FILLER                   PIC X(87) VALUE SPACES.
000780
000790   01   DETAIL2.
000800        05   FILLER                   PIC X(36) VALUE SPACES.
000810        05   DTL-LINE                 PIC X(80) VALUE SPACES.
000820        05   FILLER                   PIC X(16) VALUE SPACES.
000830
000840        EXEC SQL INCLUDE SQLCA END-EXEC.
000850
000860        EJECT
000870   PROCEDURE DIVISION.
000880
000890        PERFORM 0000-INITIALIZE.
000900
000910        READ STMTFILE INTO STMT-BUFFER
000920                  AT END MOVE '1' TO EOF-SWITCH.
000930        PERFORM 1000-PROCESS-INPUT UNTIL EOF.
000940        PERFORM 3000-TERMINATE.
000950
000960        GOBACK.
000970
000980   0000-INITIALIZE.
000990   *--------------
001000
001010        OPEN INPUT   STMTFILE
001020             OUTPUT OUTFILE.
001030
001040        MOVE '0'   TO EOF-SWITCH.
001050        MOVE SPACES TO OUT-PRT.
001060
001070   1000-PROCESS-INPUT.
001080   *------------------
001090
001100        MOVE SPACES      TO STMTD.
001110        ADD 1 TO INREC.
001120
001130        UNSTRING STMT-BUFFER DELIMITED BY ';'
001140             INTO STMTD COUNT IN STMTL.
001150
001160        EXEC SQL
001170            EXECUTE IMMEDIATE   :STMT-AREA
001180            END-EXEC.
001190
001200        IF SQLCODE EQUAL TO ZERO
```

Fig. 9.1   *(Continued)*

```
001210              ADD 1 TO OUTREC
001220         ELSE
001230              PERFORM 2000-ERROR-PRINT.
001240
001250         READ STMTFILE INTO STMT-BUFFER
001260                    AT END MOVE '1' TO EOF-SWITCH.
001270
001280   2000-ERROR-PRINT.
001290 *----------------
001300
001310         MOVE '***** STATEMENT ERROR       :' TO MSSG.
001320         MOVE SQLCODE                       TO CODE.
001330         MOVE DETAIL1      TO OUT-PRT.
001340         PERFORM 2500-LINE-PRINT.
001350
001360         MOVE FIELD1           TO DTL-LINE.
001370         MOVE DETAIL2          TO OUT-PRT.
001380         PERFORM 2500-LINE-PRINT.
001390
001400         MOVE FIELD2           TO DTL-LINE.
001410         MOVE DETAIL2          TO OUT-PRT.
001420         PERFORM 2500-LINE-PRINT.
001430
001440   2500-LINE-PRINT.
001450 *---------------
001460
001470         IF LYNES IS GREATER THAN 57
001480             WRITE OUT-REC AFTER ADVANCING NEW-PAGE
001490             MOVE 1 TO LYNES
001500         ELSE
001510             ADD 1 TO LYNES
001520             WRITE OUT-REC AFTER ADVANCING 1.
001530
001540   3000-TERMINATE.
001550 *--------------
001560
001570         MOVE '***** TOTAL RECORDS READ     :' TO MSSG.
001580         MOVE INREC        TO CODE.
001590         MOVE DETAIL1      TO OUT-PRT.
001600         WRITE OUT-REC AFTER ADVANCING NEW-PAGE.
001610
001620         MOVE '***** TOTAL RECORDS PROCESSED:' TO MSSG.
001630         MOVE OUTREC       TO CODE .
001630         MOVE DETAIL1      TO OUT-PRT.
001650         WRITE OUT-REC AFTER ADVANCING 1.
001660
001670         CLOSE STMTFILE
001680               OUTFILE.
```

Fig. 9.1   *(Continued)*

put SQL statements can be executed dynamically. The PL/1 version of the same program can be found in Appendix B.

The sample program using dynamic SQL in Figure 9.1 is very similar to other sample programs using static SQL shown in previous chapters. The only difference is the existence of the EXECUTE IMMEDIATE statement which tells us that the program is using dynamic SQL. The records in the STMTFILE file that contain SQL statements to be executed dynamically can be as follows:

INSERT INTO TEST.PATIENT (PATNAME,PATNO,SEX) VALUES

```
('KELLY','0050','F');
UPDATE TEST.PHYSICIAN SET SALARY = SALARY + (SALARY *0.07);
DELETE TEST.VISIT WHERE ADDATE '850101';
DELETE TEST.PATIENT WHERE PATNO = '0061';
DELETE TEST.VISIT WHERE IDNO = '0061';
. . .
. . .
. . .
etc.
```

9.2.2 The PREPARE statement

All the non-SELECT statements input into the program in Figure 9.1 are in the form of a string constant. Suppose we want to delete all the rows in the VISIT table from a list of patient IDs; we would have to create a record in the STMTFILE file containing a DELETE statement for each patient ID we want to delete. Whereas using static SQL, we can just use one DELETE statement within a loop and a host variable as a parameter in the WHERE clause containing a patient ID number. As the program goes through the loop, we can substitute a different patient ID number into the host variable until the end of the list. The EXECUTE IMMEDIATE statement does not allow us to substitute a host variable into the statement input buffer. However, in dynamic SQL, DB2 does allows us to parameterize or substitute the value of a host variable into our SQL statement with the use of a PRE-PARE statement followed by an EXECUTE statement. The PRE-PARE statement takes an SQL statement in the form of a character string and prepares it for execution. Its format is as follows:

```
PREPARE statement-name
    FRROM string-expression or host-variable
```

The PREPARE statement is used to prepare an SQL statement to be executed dynamically by an application program. When DB2 encounters a PREPARE statement, it creates an executable SQL statement for the statement specified in the FROM clause and assigns it a name. If the name assigned to a prepared statement is the same as the name of a previously prepared statement, the previously prepared statement will be destroyed or no longer valid for execution. SQL statements to be prepared contain a question mark (?) where the value of a host variable is to be substituted.

Example 9.1   Suppose the host variable STMT-AREA in our program contains the string DELETE TEST.VISIT WHERE IDNO = ? and we want to prepare it and call it THIS. We can code the PREPARE statement in our program as follows:

```
EXEC SQL PREPARE this
    FROM :stmt-area
   END-EXEC.
```

As with the EXECUTE IMMEDIATE statement, we cannot use the following SQL statements with the PREPARE statement: CLOSE, DECLARE, DESCRIBE, EXECUTE, FETCH, INCLUDE, OPEN, PREPARE, and WHENEVER. Each SQL statement needs to be prepared only once, and it can be executed as many times as needed. The use of a question mark (?) to parameterize our SQL statements has the following restrictions:

1. A question mark cannot be both operands of a single arithmetic operator or appear on both sides of a comparison operator. The following statements would be invalid if we tried to prepare them as in Example 9.1:

    ```
    'DELETE TEST.PHYSICIAN WHERE ( ? /? ) > 5000'
    ```

    or

    ```
    'DELETE TEST.VISIT WHERE ? = ?'
    ```

2. A question mark cannot appear as the first and second operand when the keywords BETWEEN or IN are used. We cannot prepare the following statements:

    ```
    'DELETE TEST.PHYSICIAN WHERE ? BETWEEN ? AND 50000'
    ```

    or

    ```
    'DELETE TEST.VISIT WHERE ? IN ( ?,'612','345')'
    ```

But we can prepare the following statements:

```
'DELETE TEST.PHYSICIAN WHERE salary BETWEEN ? AND ?'
```

or

```
'DELETE TEST.VISIT WHERE mdno IN ( ?,?,'345')'
```

3. Since a SELECT statement can also be prepared, a question mark cannot appear in the select list. We will discuss SELECT statements in dynamic SQL in later sections. The following statement cannot be prepared:

    ```
    'SELECT ? FROM PHYSICIAN WHERE salary BETWEEN 40000 AND 50000'
    ```

9.2.3 The DECLARE STATEMENT statement

The DECLARE STATEMENT statement is used to declare one or more names to be used by the PREPARED statements in our application program. The general format of the DECLARE STATEMENT

statement is as follows:

```
DECLARE statement-name ,
      . . .              ,
        statement name   STATEMENT
```

In a Cobol application program, all DECLARE statements must be coded in the working-storage section. The use of the DECLARE STATEMENT statement is shown in Example 9.2.

9.2.4   The EXECUTE statement

The EXECUTE statement is used execute an SQL statement after it has been prepared. The format of the EXECUTE statement can be as follows:

```
EXECUTE statement-name
  USING host-variable,
      . . .              ,
    host-variable
```

Example 9.2   Instead of showing a whole program as in Figure 9.1, we will only show the SQL statements needed to use non-SELECT parameterized SQL statements in dynamic SQL. They are as follows:

```
ID DIVISION.
  . . .
  . . .
ENVIRONMENT DIVISION.
  . . .
  . . .
DATA DIVISION.
  . . .
  . . .
WORKING-STORAGE SECTION.
  . . .
  . . .
  . . .
01 FIELD1       PIC X(4) VALUE SPACES.

01 STMT-AREA.
  49 STMTL      PIC S9(4) COMP.
  49 STMTD      PIC X(160) VALUE SPACES.

  EXEC SQL INCLUDE SQLCA END-EXEC.

  EXEC SQL DECLARE THIS STATEMENT END-EXEC.
  . . .
  . . .
  . . .
PROCEDURE DIVISION.
  . . .
  . . .
  . . . read an input record containing an SQL . . . statement to be
```

```
      prepared into a statement buffer.
 ...move the statement into the statement area (i.e., STMT-AREA)
 ...verify that the statement can be prepared.
EXEC SQL
  PREPARE THIS
    FROM :STMT-AREA
  END-EXEC.
 ...
 ...
 ...check the SQLCA to see if the statement has been prepared
    successfully.
 ...
 ...
 ...read one or more values into one or more host variables
    to be substituted (i.e., FIELD1).
 ...perform inner loop until FIELD1 is not empty.
INNER-LOOP.
  EXEC SQL
    EXECUTE THIS
      USING :FIELD1
    END-EXEC.
   ...
   ...check the SQLCA to see if the statement has been executed
      successfully.
   ...
   ...
   ...read next value into FIELD1 to be substituted.
   ...
   ...
```

The SQL statements shown in Example 9.2 are fairly straightforward since we deal only with non-SELECT statements. All we have to do is to prepare an SQL statement once and execute it as many times as we want with different values of the host variable.

9.3 Executing SELECT Statements Dynamically

Dealing with non-SELECT statements dynamically is fairly simple, since non-SELECT statements do not return any data to the application program. But when our application program is to process SELECT statements dynamically, we must consider two cases: when all the SELECT statements to be processed by our program will return the same number of data items with specific data types and when the number of data items and their data types returned by the SELECT statements in our program are not predictable. We have Fixed-List SELECT statements in the first case and Varying-List SELECT statements in the second.

9.3.1 Fixed-List SELECT statements

Suppose we have an application program that processes SELECT statements dynamically and we know that all the SELECT statements input to our program will return two fields to it. We also know that the first field is a 4-byte character string and the second one is a 6-byte character string. Since the number of fields returned and their data types are known, we can predefine in our program all the necessary host variables to contain them with Fixed-List SELECT statements as shown in Example 9.3.

Example 9.3 As in Example 9.2, we will only show the necessary statements in the program; they are:

```
ID DIVISION.
    . . .
    . . .
ENVIRONMENT DIVISION.
    . . .
    . . .
DATA DIVISION.
    . . .
    . . .
WORKING-STORAGE SECTION.
    . . .
    . . .
01 STMT-AREA.
    49 STMTL      PIC S9(4) COMP.
    49 STMTD      PIC X(160) VALUE SPACES.
01 FIELD1         PIC X(4) VALUE SPACES.
01 FIELD2         PIC X(6) VALUE SPACES.
    . . .
    . . .
    EXEC SQL INCLUDE SQLCA END-EXEC.

    EXEC SQL DECLARE THIS STATEMENT END-EXEC.

    EXEC SQL DECLARE P1 CURSOR FOR THIS
        END-EXEC.
  PROCEDURE DIVISION.
    . . .
    . . .
    . . . read an input record containing an SQL statement to be
        prepared into a statement buffer.
    . . . move the statement into the statement area (i.e., STMT-AREA).
    . . . verify that the statement can be prepared.

    EXEC SQL
    PREPARE THIS
      FROM :STMT-AREA
        END-EXEC.

    EXEC SQL OPEN P1 END-EXEC.
```

```
EXEC SQL FETCH P1 INTO :FIELD1, :FIELD2
  END-EXEC.
...
...
...process returned data items.
...etc.
...
...loop back to get next row.
...
...
EXEC SQL CLOSE P1 END-EXEC.
...
...loop back to read next input record.
...
```

The SELECT statements input into the program in Example 9.3 are as follows:

```
SELECT IDNO,ADDATE FROM TEST.VISIT WHERE MDNO = '234';
SELECT IDNO,ADDATE FROM TEST.VISIT WHERE ADDATE > '860000';
```

Using the dynamic SQL, we cannot embed host variables within SQL statements. Thus, we have to declare a cursor for our SELECT statement. The only extra step we have take in the program in Example 9.3 is to prepare the statement before we can declare a cursor for it.

9.3.2   Varying-List SELECT statements

When our application program processes SELECT statements dynamically and the number of data items and the data types returned are not known in advance, we cannot predefine the host variables to hold those values. Therefore, before the statement is executed in our program, DB2 needs to pass some information about the SQL statement to it so that we can allocate enough storage areas to hold the result of our query.

SQL descriptor area. We know that the SQL Communication Area (SQLCA) is an area used by DB2 to pass information about the result of our SQL statement to our program. The SQL Descriptor Area (SQLDA) is another area used by DB2 to store information about an SQL statement before it is executed. Application programs processing Varying-List SELECT statements are required to use the SQLDA in order to execute them dynamically. Our application program uses the information in the SQLDA to dynamically allocate storage areas to hold the result of our query at run time. For this reason, programs using Varying-List SELECT statements are written in PL/1 but not in Cobol, because the Cobol language does not support pointer variables and dynamic storage allocation. Cobol programs cannot run without an Assembler subroutine to manage the storage allocation. Because of the restrictions of Cobol, the rest of the examples in this chapter will be given in PL/1. The SQLDA is a based structure allocated at run time. To use it in our program, we can either hard code it or use an INCLUDE statement as follows:

```
EXEC SQL INCLUDE SQLDA;
```

With the INCLUDE statement, the precompiler will expand the structure as follows:

```
DCL 1 SQLDA BASED(SQLDAPTR),
      2 SQLDAID      CHAR(8),
      2 SQLDABC      BIN FIXED(31),
      2 SQLDN        BIN FIXED,
      2 SQLD         BIN FIXED,
      2 SQLVAR       (SQLSIZE REFER(SQLN)),
        3 SQLTYPE    BIN FIXED,
        3 SQLLEN     BIN FIXED,
        3 SQLDATA    PTR,
        3 SQLIND     PTR,
        3 SQLNAME    CHAR(30) VAR ;
DCL SQLSIZE BIN FIXED ;
DCL SQLDAPTR PTR ;
```

When we code the structure ourselves, we can use any name we want. Actually, the SQLDA serves two purposes depending the SQL statement it is used with. Besides giving the application program information about each SQL statement, it can also be used to pass information about host variables that we need to define when we want to parameterize our SQL statement.

We must allocate the storage for each SQL descriptor area at run time before we can use it. Notice that each descriptor area has a fixed 16-byte header of four fields: SQLAID, SQLDABC, SQLN, and SQLD. The rest of the descriptor area is an array of the substructure called SQLVAR which consists of five variables: SQLTYPE, SQLLEN, SQLDATA, SQLIND, and SQLNAME. Each SQLVAR is 44 bytes long and is repeated SQLN number of times, depending on the value we assign to SQLN. Each SQLVAR is used to store information about each column returned in the result table. The storage required for each SQL descriptor area can be calculated as follows:

$$\text{SQLDA size (in bytes)} = 16 \text{ bytes} + (\text{SQLN} \times 44 \text{ bytes})$$

The DESCRIBE statement.   After an SQL statement has been prepared, we have to issue a DESCRIBE statement so that DB2 can pass information about the prepared statement to our program before we can define a cursor for it. The general format of the DESCRIBE statement can be as follows:

```
DESCRIBE statement-name
    INTO descriptor-name
```

The statement name is the name we give to the prepared statement, and the descriptor name is the name of the SQL descriptor area.

Example 9.4   This example shows some of the statements used in a PL/1 program using Varying-List SELECT statements. They are:

```
. . .
. . .
EXEC SQL INCLUDE SQLCA;

EXEC SQL INCLUDE SQLDA;

EXEC SQL DECLARE THIS STATEMENT ;

EXEC SQL DECLARE P1 CURSOR FOR THIS ;

DCL 1 BUFFER__AREA BASED(AREAPTR),
  2 AREALEN         BIN FIXED(15),
  2 IO__AREA        (AREASIZE REFER(AREALEN))
                    CHAR(1);
DCL AREASIZE        BIN FIXED(15) INIT(0);
DCL AREAPTR         PTR;
DCL OFFSET          BIN FIXED(31);
  . . .
  . . .
...allocate storage for buffer area (use multiple number of page
size, usually 4096 bytes).
AREASIZE  = AREASIZE + 4096 - 2 ;
ALLOCATE BUFFER__AREA ;
  . . .
...point the beginning of the SQL descriptor area to the beginning of
the I/O area.
SQLDAPTR = ADDR(IO__AREA);
...allocate a storage of 16 + (10 *44) = 456 bytes to the SQLDA.
SQLSIZE  = 10;

...read an input record containing an SQL statement to be prepared
into a statement buffer.
DO WHILE (:EOF);
    ...move the statement into the statement area (STMT-AREA).
    ...verify that the statement can be prepared.

    EXEC SQL PREPARE THIS FROM :STMT-AREA;

EXEC SQL DESCRIBE THIS INTO SQLDA;

IF SQLD > SQLN THEN DO;
  SQLN = SQLD;
  EXEC SQL DESCRIBE THIS INTO SQLDA;
  END;
  . . .
  . . .
...first available address after the SQL descriptor area.
OFFSET = 16 + (SQLD × 44) + 1 ;

DO I = 1 TO SQLD ;
```

```
        . . .
        . . .
        . . . check fields SQLTYPE and SQLLEN to see what data type the col-
        umn has and also if null is allowed.
        . . . determine the length of the column and store it as a variable
        (i.e., COLEN).
        . . . if null is allowed, store the value 2 to a variable (i.e.,
        IND); otherwise store 0 to it.
        . . .
        IF IND > 0 THEN
          SQLIND (I)  = ADDR (IO__AREA(OFFSET)) ;
        SQLDATA (I) = ADDR (IO_AREA(OFFSET + IND)) ;
        OFFSET      = OFFSET + COLEN + IND ;
  END;
  . . .
  . . .
  EXEC SQL OPEN P1 ;

  EXEC SQL FETCH P1 USING DESCRIPTOR SQLDA ;

  DO WHILE (SQLCODE = 0);
        . . .
        . . .
        DO J = 1 TO SQLD ;
        . . .
        . . . get each column name returned from SQLVAR.
        . . .
        . . . get the value of each column returned
        . . . by calculating the offset address using SQLTYPE and SQLLEN as
        in previous step.
        . . .
        . . . process each column returned.
        . . .
        END;
        . . .
        . . .
        . . .
        EXEC SQL FETCH P1 USING DESCRIPTOR SQLDA ;
        END;

        EXEC SQL CLOSE P1 ;
        . . .
        . . . read next input record containing an SQL statement to be prepared
        into a statement buffer.
        . . .
END;
```

When a DESCRIBE statement is executed in our program, DB2 puts the following information in the corresponding SQL descriptor area:

SQLDAID contains the value SQLDA.

SQLDABC contains the length of the SQL descriptor area [16 + (44 × SQLN)].

SQLD contains the number of columns in the result table if the prepared statement is a SELECT statement. For non-SELECT statements SQLD will have the value of zero.

The value in SQLD can serve two purposes: If, after a DESCRIBE is executed, the value of SQLD is zero, we know it is a non-SELECT statement and we can issue an EXECUTE statement to process it. Otherwise, if the value of SQLD is greater than zero, we can compare it to the value we assign to SQLN to see if we have allocated enough storage for the SQL descriptor area. If SQLD is greater than SQLN, the size of the SQL descriptor area allocated is not large enough to hold the description of all the returned columns. We need to increase the size of our SQL descriptor area and reissue the DESCRIBE statement.

When a prepared statement is successfully described, DB2 puts an entry in the SQLVAR array for each column returned in the SELECT statement. In other words, the first column in the select list corresponds to the first SQLVAR entry, the second column corresponds to the second entry, etc. For each SQLVAR entry, the field SQLTYPE contains a three-digit code specifying the data type of the column. Some of the three-digit codes of the SQLTYPE are as follows:

Code	Data type	Null allowed
448	VARCHAR	NO
449	VARCHAR	YES
452	CHAR	NO
453	CHAR	YES
...	...	...
...	...	...
496	INTEGER	NO
497	INTEGER	YES

There is a complete list of the SQLTYPE codes in Appendix F of the *IBM DB2 Reference Manual*. The field SQLLEN contains the length of the column and is dependent on the data type of it. If the column is SMALLINT, INTEGER, or FLOAT, the value of SQLLEN is 2, 4, or 8, respectively. For the CHAR or VARCHAR column, SQLLEN contains the maximum length of the string. For columns with decimal data, SQLLEN contains the precision in the first byte and the scale in the second. The field SQLNAME contains the name of the column.

With all the information about each column to be retrieved stored as an entry in the SQLVAR, the application program has to allocate a storage area and then set the value of SQLDATA to point to that area. If a column also allows null, a 2-byte storage area must be allocated and the field SQLIND must be set to point to it. For each row returned, the value of each column will be stored in the area pointed to by the corresponding SQLDATA. If a column allows null, a value will be stored in the area pointed to by the corresponding SQLIND. A zero value means that the returned value of the related column is not null, a negative value specifies that the returned value is null, and a positive value means that the returned value has been truncated because of insufficient storage allocation; that value is also the full length of the column.

After all the storage areas have been allocated, the coding of the program looks very much as though we used static SQL. However, in the FETCH statement, we must specify the SQL descriptor area which contains the address of the storage areas to which the results will be returned. Unlike the SQLCA, we can have more than one SQLDA in our program if we have more than one cursor opened at a time. Each SQL descriptor area will point to a different storage area.

We will conclude this chapter with an example showing the layout of the SQL descriptor area and other storage areas after the FETCH statement of a program such as is in Example 9.4 has executed.

Example 9.5 Suppose we code a program such as the one in Example 9.4. A SELECT statement is read into the program as follows:

```
SELECT PATNO,BIRTHDATE FROM TEST.PATIENT WHERE PATNO =   '0001';
```

After the FETCH statement is executed, the storage area pointed to by the SQL descriptor area can be pictured as in Figure 9.2.

The areas in rectangular boxes in the figure are assumed to be contiguous areas of main storage. The first four values, SQLDA, 456, 10, and 2, represent the values of the first four fields in the header of the SQL descriptor area: SQLAID, SQLABC, SQLN, and SQLD. Since

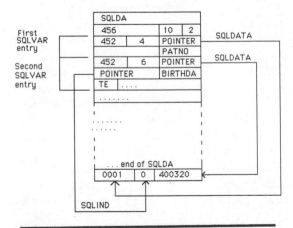

Fig. 9.2 Storage area pointed SQLDA.

PATNO is the first column in the select list, it is represented by the first entry of the SQLVAR array. PATNO is defined to DB2 as a 4-byte (SQLLEN = 4) character (SQLTYPE = 452) column. The value of PATNO is 0001; thus its SQLDATA is pointed to the storage area where the value 0001 is stored. Since null is not allowed in PATNO, its SQLIND is pointed to any storage area. Similarly, the column BIRTHDATE has SQLTYPE equal to 452, SQLLEN equal to 6, and SQLDATA pointed to a storage area with value 400320. Since null is allowed in the column BIRTHDATE, its SQLIND is pointed to an area with a value 0, specifying that the returned value is not null.

Chapter 10

Query Optimization and DB2 Security

Normally, as users or application programmers, we are not very concerned about the cost of using system resources to get the results for our queries. Since SQL is a very powerful and flexible language, there is always more than one way to code our SELECT statements to obtain the same result. However, the cost and efficiency of each form of our SELECT statement is not the same, especially when we deal with large tables (10,000 rows or more) and complicated queries. In this chapter, we will look at some forms of SELECT statements that provide better performance than others, the rest of the DB2 utilities, and DB2 security mechanisms. We'll also briefly discuss the Query Management Facility, which is an interactive tool designed for DB2 end users.

10.1 Accessing Tables through DB2 Index

As we've seen in Chapter 8, in a large table it is very costly to scan each row sequentially; we should make use of the DB2 index whenever possible. In order for DB2 to use the index, the table it's accessing must have one or more indexes already defined. Since we do not specify anything in our SQL statements to tell DB2 when to use the index or when not to use it, it is the form of our SQL statements that DB2 uses to determine the path to get to the requested data.

10.1.1 The EXPLAIN statement

When we retrieve data from large tables with complicated search criteria, it is helpful to know if DB2 makes use of the existing index or if we need to define a new index to improve the system performance.

With the EXPLAIN statement, we can obtain all the information about the efficiency of an SQL statement. The general format of the EXPLAIN statement is as follows:

```
EXPLAIN PLAN/ALL
    SET QUERYNO = integer
    FOR sql-statement
```

Example 10.1   We want to know all the information about the access path of a SELECT statement that retrieves data from the VISIT table. The code is as follows:

```
EXPLAIN PLAN FOR
    SELECT idno, addate FROM TEST.VISIT WHERE mdno = '234'
```

But before we can use the EXPLAIN statement, we must define a DB2 table named PLAN_TABLE in the database and table space we can use; we would do so as follows:

```
CREATE TABLE userid.PLAN_TABLE
```

(QUERYNO	INTEGER	NOT NULL,
QBLOCKNO	SMALLINT	NOT NULL,
APPLNAME	CHAR(8)	NOT NULL,
PROGNAME	CHAR(8)	NOT NULL,
PLANNO	SMALLINT	NOT NULL,
METHOD	SMALLINT	NOT NULL,
CREATOR	CHAR(8)	NOT NULL,
TNAME	CHAR(18)	NOT NULL,
TABNO	SMALLINT	NOT NULL,
ACCESSTYPE	CHAR(2)	NOT NULL,
MATCHCOLS	SMALLINT	NOT NULL,
ACCESSCREATOR	CHAR(8)	NOT NULL,
ACCESSNAME	CHAR(18)	NOT NULL,
INDEXONLY	CHAR(1)	NOT NULL,
SORTN_UNIQ	CHAR(1)	NOT NULL,
SORTN_JOIN	CHAR(1)	NOT NULL,
SORTN_ORDERBY	CHAR(1)	NOT NULL,
SORTN_GROUPBY	CHAR(1)	NOT NULL,
SORTC_UNIQ	CHAR(1)	NOT NULL,
SORTC_JOIN	CHAR(1)	NOT NULL,
SORTC_ORDERBY	CHAR(1)	NOT NULL,
SORTC_GROUPBY	CHAR(1)	NOT NULL,
TSLOCKMODE	CHAR(3)	NOT NULL,
TIMESTAMP	CHAR(16)	NOT NULL,
REMARKS	VARCHAR(254)	NOT NULL)

```
IN database_name.tablespace_name
```

The EXPLAIN statement can be issued interactively or can be embedded with an application program. It must be used only to explain the following SQL statements: DELETE, INSERT, SELECT, or UPDATE. When an EXPLAIN statement is executed, DB2 does not execute the explainable SQL statement that is embedded within the EXPLAIN statement, but it inserts into the PLAN_TABLE table one or more rows which contain information about the access path and the efficiency of the explainable SQL statements as though it were executed. The keyword PLAN or ALL in the EXPLAIN statement has the same meaning; it tells DB2 to insert a row into the PLAN_TABLE table for each step required to process the SQL statement.

A complicated query usually requires more than one step to process it, and each step will have a corresponding row in the PLAN_TABLE table. Therefore, each row in the PLAN_TABLE table that belongs to the same SQL statement will have the same value in the column QUERYNO. The value of the column QUERYNO is uniquely assigned by DB2, unless we explicitly assign a value to it with the clause SET QUERYNO in the EXPLAIN statement. After the EXPLAIN statement is executed, we can retrieve data from the PLAN_TABLE table to look at all the statistics of our SQL statement.

Example 10.2   Suppose we know that the value of QUERYNO is 100 for our SQL statement; we can retrieve the rows that belong to our explainable SQL statement as follows:

```
SELECT * FROM userid.PLAN_TABLE
   WHERE queryno = 100
```

In order to be able to make use of the information contained in the PLAN_TABLE table, we need to understand the purpose of each column and the values it contains. They are as follows:

Column	Usage
QUERYNO	Contains an integer; it is used to differentiate a set of rows in the PLAN_TABLE table belonging to an explainable SQL statement from another.
QBLOCKNO	Used to identify the level within an explainable SQL statement being processed; the outermost level is 1, and so on.
APPLNAME	The application plan name generated during the BIND process is stored in this column. For dynamic SQL, this column contains blanks.
PROGNAME	Contains the application program name embedded in the EXPLAIN statement.
PLANNO	Contains the step number in the application plan that corresponds to the QBLOCKNO being processed.
METHOD	Method number used in this step.
CREATOR	Contains the name of the owner of the table accessed in this step.
TNAME	Contains the name of the table accessed in this step.
TABNO	Table reference number.

ACCESSTYPE	I for new table accessed by an index; R for new table accessed by table scan.
MATCHCOLS	For ACCESSTYPE = I is number of columns of the index used to match.
ACCESSCREATOR	Creator of the index.
ACCESSNAME	Name of the index.
INDEXONLY	Y is access index only; N is data must also be accessed.
SORTN_UNIQ	(Y/N); whether a sort is performed to remove duplicate rows on a new table.
SORTN_JOIN	(Y/N); whether a sort is performed in a JOIN on a new table.
SORTN_ORDERBY	(Y/N); whether a sort is performed for an ORDER BY on a new table.
SORTN_GROUPBY	(Y/N); whether a sort is performed for a GROUP BY on a new table.
SORTC_UNIQ	(Y/N); whether a sort is performed to remove duplicate rows.
SORTC_JOIN	(Y/N); whether a sort is performed in a JOIN.
SORTC_ORDERBY	(Y/N); whether a sort is performed for an ORDER BY.
SORTC_GROUPBY	(Y/N); whether a sort is performed for a GROUP BY.
TSLOCKMODE	Lock mode on the table space of the new table.
TIMESTAMP	YYYYMMDDHHMMSSTH. Date, hour, minute, second, and tenth and hundredth of a second when the EXPLAIN statement is executed.
REMARKS	Field to be used by the user.

For more information on the meaning of the columns in the PLAN_TABLE, readers should refer to the *IBM Database2 Reference Manual*. In order to find out if DB2 tried to make the index, we should look at the value of columns ACCESSTYPE and MATCHCOLS for each step of the explainable statement processed. If the value of the column ACCESSTYPE is I and the column MATCHCOLS contains a value greater than 0, DB2 did make use of the index in that particular step.

10.2 Using SELECT statements

Sometimes when we try to retrieve data from more than one table, our SELECT statement takes longer than we expected. Perhaps we should try to rephrase our SELECT statement so that DB2 can make use of its resources more efficiently or should try to avoid using an operation that consumes a lot of system resources. In a relational database environment, one of the big consumers of system resources and time is the subquery.

Let's look at the following SELECT statement:

```
SELECT patient.patno,patient.patname
   FROM patient
  WHERE patno  IN
      ( SELECT idno
          FROM visit
        WHERE addate > '860000')
```

With the JOIN operation, DB2 only has to scan the VISIT table once to select all the rows that have a value in the column ADDATE that is greater than 860000, and for each IDNO it finds a matching PATNO in the PATIENT table. Thus, we should try to avoid the use of the subquery and use the JOIN operation whenever possible, since it is much more efficient.

As we've seen in Chapter 4, the search condition in the WHERE clause can be coded in several ways. But as a rule of thumb, the following coding habits will minimize the work needed to be done by DB2 and will thus improve the performance of our SQL statements. We should try to use them whenever possible.

Perform all numeric conversions outside the SQL statements:

Suppose we want to retrieve from the PHYSICIAN table all the physicians who earn more than $43,000 a year. Instead of coding the search condition like this:

```
...WHERE salary > 4.3E4
```

we should convert the value into decimal and code it like this:

```
...WHERE salary > 43000
```

Use the correct length for fixed-length character string comparisons:

Do not code like this:

```
...WHERE mdno = '234 '
```

but code like this, since MDNO is only a CHAR(3) column:

```
...WHERE mdno = '234'
```

Perform all arithmetic expressions outside the SQL statements as much as possible:

Suppose in our application program, we have a host variable named VAL containing a value, and we want to select all physicians in the PHYSICIAN table whose salary is greater than twice the value of

VAL. Instead of coding like this:

```
...WHERE salary > :val *2
```

we should code it like this:

```
...val = val * 2
...
...WHERE salary > :val
```

10.3   DB2 Utilities

We shall conclude this chapter with an overview of the DB2 utilities. DB2 comes with a set of utilities for database maintenance purposes. The DBA or the system programmer is usually the person who most often uses these utilities. However, as an application programmer or a user, we should be aware of the existence and the function of these utilities. Below is a list of the function of each utility; readers should refer to the *IBM Database2 Reference Manual* or consult with the DBA at their installation if an in-depth understanding of these utilities is necessary.

Utility	*Function*
CHECK	To test one or more indexes to see if they are consistent with the data
COPY	To make a "full-image copy" or an "incremental image copy" of a table space or a data set within a table space
LOAD	To load data into one or more tables in a table space or partition
MERGECOPY	To merge several image copies to make one image copy
MODIFY	To remove records from the catalog table SYSIBM.-SYSCOPY which contains information needed for recovery
RECOVER	To recover data to the current state or a previous state; it can recover from a page up to a full table space
REORG	To reorganize a table space and its indexes for better access performance
REPAIR	To replace invalid data with valid data
RUNSTATS	To gather information about space utilization in a table space or about the efficiency of an index
STOSPACE	To update the column space in the SYSIBM.SYSINDEXES, SYSIBM. SYSTABLESPACE, and SYSIBM.SYSSTO-GROUP catalog tables

10.4   DB2 Security

DB2 provides us with a security mechanism in which each user must be authorized in order to be able to use each feature of DB2. In a DB2 environment, there are two kinds of authorities: administrative and individual. Individual authorities are granted individually, whereas an individual with administrative authority will automatically be granted certain individual authorities. There are seven levels of administrative authorities as shown in Figure 10.1.

We can see from the figure that an individual with an administrative authority will have all the individual authorities within his or her domain and all the individual authorities of the included domain(s), if there are any. For example, an individual with DBCTRL authority will have all the authorities of his or her domain and all the authorities of the DBMAINT domain.

10.4.1 Levels of authority

The purpose of this section is to explain how the individual authorities are distributed among each administrative authority level. To that end, some of the DB2 system commands will be mentioned. Those system commands will not be discussed in this book because they are only used by the DBA or individuals responsible for maintaining and monitoring DB2 resources. We've seen in Figure 10.1 that there are seven levels of administrative authorities and that each level of authority possesses a number of individual authorities. Here is what those individual authorities are at each level:

DBMAINT (database maintenance) level: an individual with DBMAINT authority will have the following privileges:

CREATETAB	Create new tables
CREATETS	Create new table spaces
DISPLAYDB	Issue -DISPLAY DATABASE command
IMAGCOPY	Run the COPY and MERGECOPY utilities
STARTDB	Issue -START DATABASE command

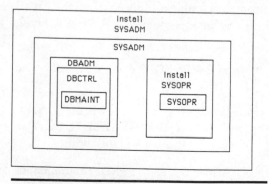

Fig. 10.1 Administrative authorities.

STATS	Run the RUNSTATS utility
STOPDB	Issue the -STOP DATABASE command

DBCTRL (database control) level: an individual with DBCTRL authority will have all the privileges of the DBMAINT level and also the following:

DROP	Drop databases
LOAD	Load tables using LOAD utility
RECOVERDB	Recover table spaces and indexes using RECOVER utility
REORG	Reorganize table spaces and indexes with REORG utility
REPAIR	Repair table spaces and indexes with REPAIR utility.

DBADM (database administration) level: an individual with DBADM authority will have all the privileges of the DBCTRL and DBMAINT levels and also the following:

ALTER	Use the ALTER statement
DELETE	Use the DELETE statement
INDEX	Use the INDEX statement
INSERT	Use the INSERT statement
SELECT	Use the SELECT statement
UPDATE	Use the UPDATE statement.

SYSOPR (system operation) level: an individual with SYSOPR authority will have the following privileges:

DISPLAY	Use the -DISPLAY THREAD and -DISPLAY DATABASE commands
RECOVER	Use the -RECOVER INDOUBT command
STOPALL	Use the -STOP DB2 command
TRACE	Use the -START TRACE and STOP TRACE commands.

Install SYSOPR (install system operation): an individual with Install SYSOPR authority will have all the privileges of the SYSOPR level, as well as the following:

IMAGCOPY	Run the COPY and MERGECOPY on DNSDB01 and DNSDB06.

SYSADM (system administration) level: an individual with SYSADM authority will have all the privileges of the DBADM, DBCTRL, DBMAINT, Install SYSOPR, SYSOPR, and also the following:

BIND	Use the BIND, REBIND, and FREE subcommands against application.plan(s)

BINDADD	Create new application plan
BSDS	Use -RECOVER BSDS command
CREATEDBA	Create new databases and have DBADM authority over them
CREATEDBC	Create new databases and have DBCTRL authority over them
CREATESG	Create new storage groups
EXECUTE	Run programs against application plan(s)
STOSPACE	Use STOSPACE utility

Install SYSADM (install system administration): an individual with Install SYSADM will have all the privileges of the SYSADM, DBADM, DBCTRL, DBMAINT, Install SYSOPR, and SYSOPR levels.

We can see that the person with Install SYSADM authority possesses the most privileges in a DB2 environment. An application programmer or a user does not have to possess any authorization to code and precompile programs accessing DB2 data. However, for each function we want to perform such as retrieving DB2 data, binding and executing programs, etc., we need to have those privileges granted to us. In a DB2 environment, the GRANT and REVOKE statements are used to give and remove individual authority to and from DB2 users.

10.4.2 The GRANT statement

The GRANT statement is used to grant privileges to DB2 users. The privileges are classified into five categories: database, plan, system, table, and use. Therefore, there are five formats of the GRANT statement, each of which can be issued interactively or can be embedded within an application program.

Grant database privileges. The format of the GRANT statement to grant privileges from databases is as follows:

```
GRANT individual-authority [, . . ., individual-authority ]
   ON DATABASE database-name [, . . ., database-name ]
   TO authorization-id/PUBLIC [, . . ., authorization-id ]
   WITH GRANT OPTION
```

With this format, we can grant one or more individual authorities on several databases to one or more users. We can specify one or more individual authorities from the DBCTRL and DBMAINT levels. We can also use the keywords DBMAINT, DBCTRL, or DBADM to give all the privileges of the DBMAINT, DBTRL, or DBADM authority level to an individual. Notice that the person with DBADM authority will also have all the authorities on all DB2 objects within the database(s) that he or she has control over. Instead of listing each user ID separately, we can use the keyword PUBLIC to specify all users. When users are granted the WITH GRANT OPTION, they can then grant any privileges they have to other users.

Example 10.3   To grant create table privileges on database DBTST100 to all users, grant drop privileges on databases DBTST100 and DBTST200 to user SMITH and JOHNSON, and to grant database control privileges to user BERG with all the privileges on databases DBTST100 and DBTST200, use the following format:

```
GRANT CREATETAB ON DATABASE dbtst100
    TO PUBLIC
GRANT DROP ON DATABASE dbtst100, dbtst200
  TO smith, johnson
GRANT DBCTRL ON DATABASE dbtst100, dbtst200
  TO berg WITH GRANT OPTION
```

Grant plan privileges.   This format of the GRANT statement is used to grant privileges to application plans:

```
GRANT BIND [ ,EXECUTE ]
    ON PLAN plan-name [ , . . . , plan-name ]
      TO authorization-id/PUBLIC [ , . . . , authorization-id ]
    WITH GRANT OPTION
```

The keyword BIND is used when we want to grant users the privileges to BIND and REBIND their application program against existing application plans. The keyword EXECUTE allows the user to run application programs against application plans specified.

Example 10.4   Grant BIND and EXECUTE privileges to SMITH with all the privileges on plan DBPL100 and DBPL200 and grant EXECUTE privilege to PUBLIC on plan DBPL100 as follows:

```
GRANT BIND, EXECUTE ON PLAN dbpl100, dbpl200
    TO smith WITH GRANT OPTION

GRANT EXECUTE ON PLAN dbpl100
    TO PUBLIC
```

Grant system privileges.   To grant system privileges with this format, we can use any individual authorities in the SYSADM and SYSOPR authority levels, except the BIND and EXECUTE authorities, which are used to grant PLAN privileges. We can also use the keywords SYSADM and SYSOPR to give all the privileges belonging to those levels. The format is as follows:

```
GRANT individual-authority [ , . . . , individual-authority ]
    TO authorization-id/PUBLIC [ , . . . , authorization-id ]
    WITH GRANT OPTION
```

Example 10.5   To grant privileges to create new databases with DBADM authority and to create new storage groups to JOE, grant create application plans to all users, and grant SYSADM privileges to JEFF with the privilege to grant system privileges to others; use the following format:

```
GRANT CREATEDBA, CREATESG
    TO joe

GRANT BINDADD
    TO PUBLIC

GRANT SYSADM
    TO jeff WITH GRANT OPTION
```

Grant table privileges.   This format of GRANT is used to grant privileges on tables and views. It is used as follows:

```
GRANT ALL /ALL PRIVILEGES
    ON [ TABLE ] table-name/view-name [, ..., table-name/view-name]
    TO authorization-id/PUBLIC [, ..., authorization-id ]
    WITH GRANT OPTION
```

or

```
GRANT [ ALTER, DELETE, INDEX, INSERT, SELECT, UPDATE,
    UPDATE ( column-name [, [ ..., column-name ] ) ]
    ON [ TABLE ] table-name/view-name [, ..., table-name/view-name]
    TO authorization-id/PUBLIC [, ..., authorization-id ]
    WITH GRANT OPTION
```

As with other formats, we can grant one or more individual privileges with this one. We can use the keyword ALL or ALL PRIVILEGES to specify all the privileges (i.e., ALTER, DELETE, INDEX, INSERT, SELECT, and UPDATE). For the UPDATE privilege, we can specify just the columns for which we want the user to have update privileges. The keyword ON or ON TABLE is used to list one or more table or view names on which the privileges are granted.

Example 10.6   To grant all table privileges on tables PATIENT and VISIT to SMITH with all the privileges and grant SELECT and UPDATE privileges on columns PATNAME, ADDRESS, and BIRTHDATE on PATIENT table to all users, use the following:

```
GRANT ALL PRIVILEGES
    ON patient, visit
    TO smith
    WITH GRANT OPTION

GRANT SELECT, UPDATE (patname, address, birthdate)
    ON patient
    TO PUBLIC
```

When using the UPDATE(column-name,...) clause, we must remember that it is not valid to use it with the WITH GRANT OPTION and also that if more than one table is specified in the ON clause, each column name listed in the UPDATE clause must belong to every table in the ON clause.

Grant use privileges. With this format, we can grant privileges to use either the BUFFERPOOL, STOGROUP, or TABLESPACE:

```
GRANT USE OF BUFFERPOOL [ BP0, BP1, BP2, BP32K ]
   TO authorization-id/PUBLIC [, ..., authorization-id ]
   WITH GRANT OPTION
```

or

```
GRANT USE OF STOGROUP storagegroup-name [, ..., storagegroup-name ]
   TO authorization-id/PUBLIC [, ..., authorization-id ]
   WITH GRANT OPTION
```

or

```
GRANT USE OF TABLESPACE tablespace-name [, ..., tablespace-name ]
   TO authorization-id/PUBLIC [, ..., authorization-id ]
   WITH GRANT OPTION
```

When granting privileges on one or more table spaces, we can either list each table space name alone or qualify them with the database name.

Example 10.7   To grant privileges to use table space TBLS100 to all users, use the following:

```
GRANT USE OF TABLESPACE dbtst100.tblsp100
   TO PUBLIC.
```

10.4.3 The REVOKE statement

After one or more privileges have been granted to a user, they can also be taken away with the REVOKE statement. The REVOKE statement can be used interactively or can be embedded within an application program. Like the GRANT statement, the REVOKE statement has one format for each privilege category (i.e., database, Plan, System, Table, and Use).

Revoke database privileges.   The format is as follows:

```
REVOKE individual-authority [, ..., individual-authority ]
   ON DATABASE database-name [, ..., database-name ]
   FROM authorization-id/PUBLIC [, ..., authorization-id ]
   [BY authorization-id/ALL [, ..., authorization-id ]]
```

In a way similar to the first format of the GRANT statement, we can use any of the following individual authorities: CREATETAB, CREATETS, DROP, DISPLAYDB, IMAGCOPY, STARTDB, STATS, STOPDB, LOAD, RECOVERDB, REORG, and REPAIR. We can also use the keywords DBADM, DBCTRL, and DBMAINT. The FROM clause is used to list the user IDs from which the privileges are revoked. The BY clause is used to list the IDs of the users who granted the specified privileges to the users named in the FROM clause. The BY clause can only be used by an individual with SYSADM authority; as a user, we must omit the BY clause and can only revoke privileges from other users if those privileges have been granted by us. The keyword ALL in the BY clause is used if the SYSADM wants to revoke explicit privileges from one or more users regardless of who granted them.

Example 10.8   To revoke create new tables privileges on database DBTST100 from all users and revoke drop privilege on databases DBTST100 and DBTST200 from SMITH and JOHNSON, use the following:

```
REVOKE CREATETAB ON DATABASE dbtst100
    FROM PUBLIC

REVOKE DROP ON DATABASE dbtst100, dbtst200
    FROM smith, johnson
```

Revoke plan privileges.   The format for this is:

```
REVOKE BIND [ ,EXECUTE ]
    ON PLAN plan-name [ , . . . , plan-name ]
FROM authorization-id/PUBLIC [ , . . . , authorization-id ]
    [BY authorization-id/ALL [ , . . . , authorization-id ]]
```

Example 10.9   Revoke BIND and EXECUTE privileges from SMITH on plan DBPL100 and DBPL200 and revoke EXECUTE privilege from all users on plan DBPL100 as follows:

```
REVOKE BIND, EXECUTE ON PLAN dbpl100, dbpl200
    FROM smith WITH GRANT OPTION

REVOKE EXECUTE ON PLAN dbpl100
    FROM PUBLIC
```

Revoke system privileges.   The format for this is:

```
REVOKE individual-authority [ , . . . , individual-authority ]
    FROM authorization-id/PUBLIC [ , . . . , authorization-id ]
        [BY authorization-id/ALL [ , . . . , authorization-id ]]
```

Example 10.10   Revoke create new databases privileges with DBADM authority and create new storage groups from JOE and revoke create application plans from all users as follows:

```
REVOKE CREATEDBA, CREATESG
    FROM joe

REVOKE BINDADD
    FROM PUBLIC
```

Revoke table privileges.   The format is as follows:

```
GRANT ALL /ALL PRIVILEGES
    ON [ TABLE ] table-name/view-name [, ..., table-name/view-name]
FROM authorization-id/PUBLIC [, ..., authorization-id ]
    [BY authorization-id/ALL [, ..., authorization-id ]]
```

or

```
REVOKE [ ALTER, DELETE, INDEX, INSERT, SELECT, UPDATE,
         UPDATE ( column-name [, ..., column-name ] ) ]
    ON [ TABLE ] table-name/view-name [, ..., table-name/view-name]
  FROM authorization-id/PUBLIC [, ..., authorization-id ]
    [BY authorization-id/ALL [, ..., authorization-id ]]
```

Example 10.11   Revoke all table privileges on tables PATIENT and VISIT from SMITH with all the privileges as follows:

```
REVOKE ALL PRIVILEGES
    ON patient, visit
    FROM smith
```

Revoke use privileges.   The format is:

```
REVOKE USE OF BUFFERPOOL [ BP0, BP1, BP2, BP32K ]
FROM authorization-id/PUBLIC [, ..., authorization-id ]
  [BY authorization-id/ALL [, ..., authorization-id ]]
```

or

```
REVOKE USE OF STOGROUP storagegroup-name [, ..., storagegroup-name ]
FROM authorization-id/PUBLIC [, ..., authorization-id ]
  [BY authorization-id/ALL [, ..., authorization-id ]]
```

or

```
REVOKE USE OF TABLESPACE tablespace-name [, ..., tablespace-name ]
FROM authorization-id/PUBLIC [, ..., authorization-id ]
  [BY authorization-id/ALL [, ..., authorization-id ]]
```

Example 10.12   Revoke privileges to use table space TBLSP100 from all users as follows:

```
REVOKE USE OF TABLESPACE dbtst100.tblsp100
    FROM PUBLIC.
```

We've seen that the GRANT and REVOKE statements are used to explicitly grant privileges and remove them from users. However, some privileges can be gained without being explicitly granted with the GRANT statement; they are called implicit privileges. In Example 10.3, we explicitly granted the privilege to create new tables (CREATETAB) to all users (PUBLIC). Users, after creating their own tables, will have all the implicit privileges on their own tables such as to ALTER and DROP those tables; create INDEXES and VIEWS for them; and INSERT, UPDATE, SELECT, and DELETE rows in them. Implicit privileges possessed by a user cannot be revoked by anyone, even the SYSADM, with the REVOKE statement. The creator of the table, table space, or index, as well as the SYSADM or DBADM, can drop or alter them.

10.5 Query Management Facility

We've seen that SQL statements can be used interactively or can be embedded in a batch application program. However, in an interactive environment such as the Time Sharing Option (TSO), users can access DB2 data through an interactive tool called "Query Management Facility" (QMF). Before looking at all the features of QMF, let's look at another interactive tool called the "Interactive System Productivity Facility" (ISPF). ISPF is called a "dialogue manager" because it manages dialogues. Each dialogue is an interactive application which consists of a series of screens or panels and a program that controls the flow in which the screens appear. In fact, ISPF can manage and control any dialogue we create or supply. ISPF works in TSO. When ISPF is invoked, an ISPF panel appears, in which the user is allowed to select an option, and each option can be a user-supplied dialogue.

QMF runs under the control of ISPF as an ISPF dialogue; that means QMF can be invoked through ISPF. QMF is an interactive tool designed for end-users; we make our queries through QMF, and QMF will use the dynamic SQL facility of DB2 to request work to be done. After the processing is finished, QMF will display the result on the terminal. Once we're in QMF, we can either use SQL (structured query language) or QBE (query by example):

With SQL, we can make our queries by typing the SQL statements the way we learned before.

With QBE, a two-dimensional table is presented to us, and we make queries by entering QBE keywords underneath each column we want to process. In other words, we do not have to code our SQL statements in QBE, but QMF will build the SQL statements for us based on the QBE keywords we selected.

Query facility is not the only feature provided by QMF; it also provides us with a reporting capability which allows us to format the result into a report we want. With QMF, we can also save our SQL statements or our QMF commands and then execute them later. All the database maintenance functions can also be invoked in QMF. For detailed information on how to use QMF, readers should refer to the IBM QMF user manual.

A

DB2 CATALOG

SYSIBM.SYSCOLAUTH Table

The SYSIBM.SYSCOLAUTH table records the UPDATE privileges held by users on individual columns of a table or view.

Column name	Data type	Description
GRANTOR	CHAR(8)	Authorization ID of the user who granted the privilege.
GRANTEE	CHAR(8)	Authorization ID of the user who holds the privilege or the name of an application plan that uses the privilege.
GRANTEETYPE	CHAR(1)	Meaning: blank GRANTEE is an authorization ID P GRANTEE is an application plan
CREATOR	CHAR(8)	The authorization ID of the creator of the table or view on which the update privilege is held.
TNAME	VARCHAR(18)	The name of the table or view.
TIMESTAMP	CHAR(12)	Time at which the privilege was granted (internal time stamp format).
DATEGRANTED	CHAR(6)	Date the privilege was granted, in the form yymmdd.
TIMEGRANTED	CHAR(8)	Time the privilege was granted, in the form hhmmssth.
COLNAME	VARCHAR(18)	Name of the column to which the UPDATE privilege applies.
IBMREQD	CHAR(1)	Whether the row came from the basic machine readable material (MRM) tape: N no Y yes

SYSIBM.SYSCOLUMNS Table

The SYSIBM.SYSCOLUMNS table contains one row for every column of each table and view (including the columns of the DB2 catalog tables).

Column name	Data type	Description
NAME	VARCHAR(18)	Name of the column.
TBNAME	VARCHAR(18)	Name of the table or view which contains the column.
TBCREATOR	CHAR(8)	Authorization ID of the creator of the table or view.
COLNO	SMALLINT	Numerical place of the column in the table or view; for example, 4 (out of 10).
COLTYPE	CHAR(8)	Type of column:
		INTEGER — large integer
		SMALLINT — small integer
		FLOAT — floating-point
		CHAR — fixed-length character string
		VARCHAR — varying-length character string
		LONGVAR — varying-length character string
		DECIMAL — decimal
		GRAPHIC — fixed-length graphic string
		VARG — varying-length graphic string
		LONGVARG — varying-length graphic string
LENGTH	SMALLINT	The length attribute of the column; or, in the case of a decimal column, its precision. The number does not include the internal prefixes used to record actual length and null state where applicable.
		INTEGER — 4
		SMALLINT — 2
		FLOAT — 8
		CHAR — length of string
		VARCHAR — maximum length of string
		LONG VARCHAR — maximum length of string
		DECIMAL — precision of number
		GRAPHIC — number of DBCS characters
		VARG — maximum number of DBCS characters
		LONGVARG — maximum number of DBCS characters

Column name	Data type	Description
SCALE	SMALLINT	Scale of decimal data; zero if not a decimal column.
NULLS	CHAR(1)	Whether the column can contain null values: N no Y yes
COLCARD	INTEGER	Number of distinct values in the column. −1 if statistics have not been gathered or the column is not the first column of an index key. If the column is the first column of a key of a catalog table, the value represents a "typical catalog." For all other columns of catalog tables, the value is −1.
HIGH2KEY	CHAR(8)	Second highest value of the column. Blank if statistics have not been gathered or the column is not the first column of an index key. If the key has a noncharacter data type, the data may not be printable.
LOW2KEY	CHAR(8)	Second lowest value of the column. Blank if statistics have not been gathered or the column is not the first column of an index key. If the key has a noncharacter data type, the data may not be printable.
UPDATES	CHAR(1)	Whether the column can be updated: N no Y yes (The value is N only if the column is part of the key of a partitioned index or is derived from a function or arithmetic expression. Thus, the value can be Y for columns of a read-only view.)
IBMREQD	CHAR(1)	Whether the row came from the basic machine-readable material (MRM) tape: N no Y yes
REMARKS	VARCHAR(254)	A character string provided by the user with the COMMENT ON statement.
DEFAULT	CHAR(1)	Whether the column has a default value (null or nonnull): N no Y yes
KEYSEQ	SMALLINT	Numerical place of the column within a primary key. 0 if it is not part of a primary key. Nonzero only for columns of catalog tables.
FOREIGNKEY	CHAR(1)	Whether the column is part of a foreign key: N no Y yes (only for columns of catalog tables)

Column name	Data type	Description
FLDPROC	CHAR(1)	Whether the column has a field procedure: N no Y yes
LABEL	VARCHAR(30)	The column label as given by a LABEL ON statement; otherwise, an empty string.

SYSIBM.SYSCOPY Table

The SYSIBM.SYSCOPY table contains information needed for recovery.

Column name	Data type	Description
DBNAME	CHAR(8)	Name of the database.
TSNAME	CHAR(8)	Name of the table space.
DSNUM	INTEGER	Data set number within the table space. For partitioned table spaces, this corresponds to partition number.
ICTYPE	CHAR(1)	Operation type: F full image copy I incremental image copy P partial recovery point R LOAD REPLACE LOG(YES) W REORG LOG(NO) X REORG LOG(YES) Y LOAD LOG(NO) Z LOAD LOG(YES)
ICDATE	CHAR(6)	Date of the entry in the form yymmdd.
START_RBA	CHAR(6)	A 48-bit positive integer. For ICTYPE F or I, the starting point in the DB2 log for all updates since the image copy was taken. For other values of ICTYPE, the end of the log before the start of the RELOAD phase of the LOAD or REORG utility.
FILESEQNO	INTEGER	Tape file sequence number of the copy.
DEVTYPE	CHAR(8)	Device type the copy is on.
IBMREQD	CHAR(1)	Whether the row came from the basic machine-readable material (MRM) tape: N no Y yes
DSNAME	CHAR(44)	The name of the data set.

Column name	Data type	Description
ICTIME	CHAR(6)	Time at which the row was inserted, in the form hhmmss. Blank if rows migrated from Release 1.
SHRLEVEL	CHAR(1)	SHRLEVEL parameter on COPY (for ICTYPE F or I only): C change R reference blank does not describe an image copy or was migrated from Release 1.
DSVOLSER	VARCHAR(1784)	The volume serial numbers of the data set. A list of 6-byte numbers separated by commas.

SYSIBM.SYSDATABASE Table

The SYSIBM.SYSDATABASE table contains one row for each database, except for database DSNDB01.

Column name	Data type	Description
NAME	CHAR(8)	Database name.
CREATOR	CHAR(8)	Authorization ID of the creator of the database.
STGROUP	CHAR(8)	Name of the default storage group of the database; blank for a system database.
BPOOL	CHAR(8)	Name of the default buffer pool of the database; blank for a system database.
DBID	SMALLINT	Internal identifier of the database.
IBMREQD	CHAR(1)	Whether the row came from the basic machine-readable material (MRM) tape: N no Y yes

SYSIBM.SYSDBAUTH Table

The SYSIBM.SYSDBAUTH table records the privileges held by users for databases.

Column name	Data type	Description
GRANTOR	CHAR(8)	Authorization ID of the user who granted the privileges.
GRANTEE	CHAR(8)	Authorization ID of the user who holds the privileges, or the name of an application plan that uses the privileges.
NAME	CHAR(8)	Database name.
TIMESTAMP	CHAR(12)	Time at which the privileges were granted (internal time stamp format).
DATEGRANTED	CHAR(6)	Date the privileges were granted; in the form yymmdd.
TIMEGRANTED	CHAR(8)	Time the privileges were granted; in the form hhmmssth.
GRANTEETYPE	CHAR(1)	Meaning: blank GRANTEE is an authorization ID P GRANTEE is an application plan
AUTHHOWGOT	CHAR(1)	Authorization level of the user from whom the privileges were received: blank not applicable C DBCTL D DBADM M DBMAINT S SYSADM
CREATETABAUTH	CHAR(1)	Whether the GRANTEE can create tables within the database: blank authority is not held G authority held with the GRANT option Y authority is held without the GRANT option
CREATETSAUTH	CHAR(1)	Whether the GRANTEE can create table spaces within the database: blank authority is not held G authority held with the GRANT option Y privilege is held without the GRANT option
DBADMAUTH	CHAR(1)	Whether the GRANTEE has DBADM authority over the database: blank authority is not held G authority held with the GRANT option

Column name	Data type	Description
		Y authority is held without the GRANT option
DBCTRLAUTH	CHAR(1)	Whether the GRANTEE has DBCTRL authority over the database: blank privilege is not held G privilege held with the GRANT option Y privilege is held without the GRANT option
DBMAINTAUTH	CHAR(1)	Whether the GRANTEE has DBMAINT authority over the database: blank privilege is not held G privilege held with the GRANT option Y privilege is held without the GRANT option
DISPLAYDBAUTH	CHAR(1)	Whether the GRANTEE can issue the DISPLAY command for the database: blank privilege is not held G privilege held with the GRANT option Y privilege is held without the GRANT option
DROPAUTH	CHAR(1)	Whether the GRANTEE can drop the database: blank privilege is not held G privilege held with the GRANT option Y privilege is held without the GRANT option
IMAGCOPYAUTH	CHAR(1)	Whether the GRANTEE can use the COPY and MERGECOPY utilities on the database: blank privilege is not held G privilege held with the GRANT option Y privilege is held without the GRANT option
LOADAUTH	CHAR(1)	Whether the GRANTEE can use the LOAD utility to load tables in the database: blank privilege is not held G privilege held with the GRANT option Y privilege is held without the GRANT option
REORGAUTH	CHAR(1)	Whether the GRANTEE can use the REORG utility to reorganize table spaces and indexes in the database:

Column name	Data type	Description
		blank privilege is not held
		G privilege held with the GRANT option
		Y privilege is held without the GRANT option
RECOVERDBAUTH	CHAR(1)	Whether the GRANTEE can use the RE-COVER utility to recover table spaces of the database:
		blank privilege is not held
		G privilege held with the GRANT option
		Y privilege is held without the GRANT option
REPAIRAUTH	CHAR(1)	Whether the GRANTEE can use the RE-PAIR utility on table spaces and indexes in the database:
		blank privilege is not held
		G privilege held with the GRANT option
		Y privilege is held without the GRANT option
STARTDBAUTH	CHAR(1)	Whether the GRANTEE can use the START command against the database:
		blank privilege is not held
		G privilege held with the GRANT option
		Y privilege is held without the GRANT option
STATSAUTH	CHAR(1)	Whether the GRANTEE can use the RUNSTATS utility against the database:
		blank privilege is not held
		G privilege held with the GRANT option
		Y privilege is held without the GRANT option
STOPAUTH	CHAR(1)	Whether the GRANTEE can issue the STOP command against the database:
		blank privilege is not held
		G privilege held with the GRANT option
		Y privilege is held without the GRANT option
IBMREQD	CHAR(1)	Whether the row came from the basic machine-readable material (MRM) tape:
		N no
		Y yes

SYSIBM.SYSDBRM Table

The SYSIBM.SYSDBRM table contains one row for each DBRM of each application plan.

Column name	Data type	Description
NAME	CHAR(8)	Name of the DBRM.
TIMESTAMP	CHAR(8)	Time of precompilation in internal format.
PDSNAME	CHAR(44)	Name of the partitioned data set of which the DBRM is a member.
PLNAME	CHAR(8)	Name of the application plan of which this DBRM is a part.
PLCREATOR	CHAR(8)	Authorization ID of the creator of the application plan.
PRECOMPTIME	CHAR(8)	Time of precompilation in the form hhmmssth.
PRECOMPDATE	CHAR(6)	Date of precompilation in the form yymmdd.
QUOTE	CHAR(1)	Whether the SQL escape character is the apostrophe or the quotation mark: N apostrophe Y quotation mark
COMMA	CHAR(1)	Whether the decimal point is the period or the comma: N period Y comma
HOSTLANG	CHAR(1)	The host language used: F FORTRAN B assembler language C COBOL P PL/I
IBMREQD	CHAR(1)	Whether the row came from the basic machine-readable material (MRM) tape: N no Y yes

SYSIBM.SYSFIELDS Table

The SYSIBM.SYSFIELDS table contains one row for every column that has a field procedure.

Column name	Data type	Description
TBCREATOR	CHAR(8)	Authorization ID of the creator of the table that contains the column.
TBNAME	VARCHAR(18)	Name of the table that contains the column.
COLNO	SMALLINT	Numerical place of this column in the table.
NAME	VARCHAR(18)	Name of the column.
FLDTYPE	CHAR(8)	Data type of the encoded values in the field: INTEGER — large integer SMALLINT — small integer FLOAT — floating-point CHAR — fixed-length character string VARCHAR — varying-length character string DECIMAL — decimal GRAPHIC — fixed-length graphic string VARG — varying-length graphic string
LENGTH	SMALLINT	The length attribute of the field; or, for a decimal field, its precision. The number does not include the internal prefixes that may be used to record actual length and null state. INTEGER — 4 SMALLINT — 2 FLOAT — 8 CHAR — length of string VARCHAR — maximum length of string DECIMAL — precision of number GRAPHIC — number of DBCS characters VARG — maximum number of DBCS characters
SCALE	SMALLINT	Scale if FLDTYPE is DECIMAL; otherwise, 0.
FLDPROC	CHAR(8)	Name of the field procedure.
WORKAREA	SMALLINT	Size, in bytes, of the work area required for the encoding and decoding functions of the field procedure.

Column name	Data type	Description
IBMREQD	CHAR(1)	Whether the row came from the basic machine-readable material (MRM) tape: N no Y yes
EXITPARML	SMALLINT	Length of the field procedure parameter value block.
PARMLIST	VARCHAR(254)	The parameter list given after FIELDPROC in the statement that created the column, with insignificant blanks removed.
EXITPARM	VARCHAR(1530)	The parameter value block of the field procedure (the control block passed to the field procedure when it is invoked).

SYSIBM.SYSFOREIGNKEYS Table

The SYSIBM.SYSFOREIGNKEYS table contains one row for every column of every foreign key.

Column name	Data type	Description
CREATOR	CHAR(8)	Authorization ID of the creator of the table that contains the column.
TBNAME	VARCHAR(18)	Unqualified name of the table that contains the column.
RELNAME	CHAR(8)	Unqualified name of the link associated with the foreign key.
COLNAME	VARCHAR(18)	Name of the column.
COLNO	SMALLINT	Numerical place of the column in its table.
COLSEQ	SMALLINT	Numerical place of the column in the foreign key.
IBMREQD	CHAR(1)	Whether the row came from the basic machine-readable material (MRM) tape: N no Y yes

SYSIBM.SYSINDEXES Table

The SYSIBM.SYSINDEXES table contains one row for every index, including indexes of catalog tables.

Column name	Data type	Description
NAME	VARCHAR(18)	Name of the index.
CREATOR	CHAR(8)	Authorization ID of the creator of the index.
TBNAME	VARCHAR(18)	Name of the table on which the index is defined.
TBCREATOR	CHAR(8)	Authorization ID of the creator of the table.
UNIQUERULE	CHAR(1)	Whether the index is unique: D no (duplicates are allowed) U yes
COLCOUNT	SMALLINT	The number of columns in the key.
CLUSTERING	CHAR(1)	Whether CLUSTER was specified when the index was created: N no Y yes
CLUSTERED	CHAR(1)	Whether the table is actually clustered by the index: N no: 95% of the rows, or fewer, are in clustering order. Y yes: More than 95% of the rows are in clustering order. The entry can be changed by the RUNSTATS utility.
DBID	SMALLINT	Internal identifier of the database.
OBID	SMALLINT	Internal identifier of the index.
ISOBID	SMALLINT	Internal identifier of the index space.
DBNAME	CHAR(8)	Name of the database that contains the index.
INDEXSPACE	CHAR(8)	Name of the index space.
FIRSTKEYCARD	INTEGER	Number of distinct values of the first 8 bytes of the first key column, or of the entire column if it is narrower than 8 bytes. −1 before statistics are gathered.
FULLKEYCARD	INTEGER	Number of distinct values of the key. −1 before statistics are gathered.
NLEAF	INTEGER	Number of active leaf pages in the index. −1 before statistics are gathered.
NLEVELS	SMALLINT	Number of levels in the index tree. −1 before statistics are gathered.

Column name	Data type	Description
BPOOL	CHAR(8)	Name of the buffer pool used for the index.
PGSIZE	SMALLINT	Size of subpages in the index: 256, 512, 1024, 2048, or 4096.
ERASERULE	CHAR(1)	Whether the data sets are erased when dropped. The value is meaningless if the index is partitioned. N no Y yes
DSETPASS	CHAR(8)	The password for the data sets of the index.
CLOSERULE	CHAR(1)	Whether the data sets are closed when the index is not in use: N no Y yes
SPACE	INTEGER	Number of kilobytes of DASD storage allocated to the index, as determined by the last execution of the STOSPACE utility. The value is 0 if the index is not related to a storage group or if STOSPACE has not been run.
IBMREQD	CHAR(1)	Whether the row came from the basic machine-readable material (MRM) tape: N no Y yes

SYSIBM.SYSINDEXPART Table

The SYSIBM.SYSINDEXPART table contains one row for each unpartitioned index and one row for each partition of a partitioned index.

Column name	Data type	Description
PARTITION	SMALLINT	Partition number; 0 if index is not partitioned.
IXNAME	VARCHAR(18)	Name of the index.
IXCREATOR	CHAR(8)	Authorization ID of the creator of the index.
PQTY	INTEGER	Primary space allocation in units of 4K-byte storage blocks. Zero if a storage group is not used.
SQTY	SMALLINT	Secondary space allocation in units of 4K-byte storage blocks. Zero if a storage group is not used.

Column name	Data type	Description
STORTYPE	CHAR(1)	Type of storage allocation: E explicit and STORNAME names a VSAM catalog I implicit and STORNAME names a storage group
STORNAME	CHAR(8)	Name of storage group or VSAM catalog used for space allocation.
VCATNAME	CHAR(8)	Name of VSAM catalog used for space allocation.
CARD	INTEGER	Number of rows referenced by the index or partition. −1 if statistics not gathered.
FAROFFPOS	INTEGER	Number of referenced rows away from optimal position because of an insert into a full page. −1 if statistics not gathered.
LEAFDIST	INTEGER	100 times the average number of pages between successive leaf pages of the index. −1 if statistics not gathered.
NEAROFFPOS	INTEGER	Number of referenced rows near, but not at optimal position, because of an insert into a full page.
IBMREQD	CHAR(1)	Whether the row came from the basic machine-readable material (MRM) tape: N no Y yes
LIMITKEY	VARCHAR(512)	The limit key of the partition; 0 if the index is not partitioned.
FREEPAGE	SMALLINT	The number of pages that are loaded before a page is left as free space.
PCTFREE	SMALLINT	The percentage of each subpage or nonleaf page that is left as free space.

SYSIBM.SYSKEYS Table

The SYSIBM.SYSKEYS table contains one row for each column of an index key.

Column name	Data type	Description
IXNAME	VARCHAR(18)	Name of the index.
IXCREATOR	CHAR(8)	Authorization ID of the creator of the index.
COLNAME	VARCHAR(18)	Name of the column of the key.

Column name	Data type	Description
COLNO	SMALLINT	Numerical position of the column in the row; for example 4 (out of 10).
COLSEQ	SMALLINT	Numerical position of the column in the key; for example 4 (out of 10).
ORDERING	CHAR(1)	Order of the column in the key: A ascending D descending
IBMREQD	CHAR(1)	Whether the row came from the basic machine-readable material (MRM) tape: N no Y yes

SYSIBM.SYSLINKS Table

The SYSIBM.SYSLINKS table contains one row for every link between tables. (In each link, the parent and children are catalog tables.)

Column name	Data type	Description
CREATOR	CHAR(8)	Authorization ID of the creator of the child table of the link.
TBNAME	VARCHAR(18)	Unqualified name of the child table.
LINKNAME	CHAR(8)	Unqualified name of the link.
PARENTNAME	VARCHAR(18)	Unqualified name of the parent table of the link.
PARENTCREATOR	CHAR(8)	Authorization ID of the creator of the parent table of the link.
CHILDSEQ	SMALLINT	Cluster order of the child table within its parent table.
DBNAME	CHAR(8)	Name of the database containing the link.
DBID	SMALLINT	Internal DB2 identifier of the database.
OBID	SMALLINT	Internal DB2 identifier of the link.
COLCOUNT	SMALLINT	Number of columns in the ordering key for the link. 0 if there is no ordering key.
INSERTRULE	CHAR(1)	Type of insert rule for the link: F FIRST

Column name	Data type	Description
		L LAST O ONE U UNIQUE
IBMREQD	CHAR(1)	Whether the row came from the basic machine-readable material (MRM) tape: N no Y yes

SYSIBM.SYSPLAN Table

The SYSIBM.SYSPLAN table contains one row for each application plan.

Column name	Data type	Description
NAME	CHAR(8)	Name of the application plan.
CREATOR	CHAR(8)	Authorization ID of the creator of the application plan.
BINDDATE	CHAR(6)	Date on which the most recent BIND was performed in the form yymmdd.
VALIDATE	CHAR(1)	Whether validity checking can be deferred until run time: B all checking must be performed during BIND R checking is deferred if tables, views, or privileges do not exist at bind time
ISOLATION	CHAR(1)	The isolation level: R repeatable read S cursor stability
VALID	CHAR(1)	Whether the application plan is valid (whether it can be run without rebinding): N no Y yes
OPERATIVE	CHAR(1)	Whether the application plan can be allocated: N no; an explicit BIND or REBIND is required before the plan can be allocated Y yes
BINDTIME	CHAR(8)	Time of the BIND in the form hhmmssth.
PLSIZE	INTEGER	Size of the base section* of the plan. Used by DB2 to allocate storage for the control structure.

Column name	Data type	Description
IBMREQD	CHAR(1)	Whether the row came from the basic machine-readable material (MRM) tape: N no Y yes
AVGSIZE	INTEGER	Average size of those sections: fnref = secfn. of the plan that contains DML statements processed at bind time.
ACQUIRE	CHAR(1)	When resources are acquired: A at allocation U at first use
RELEASE	CHAR(1)	When resources are released: C at commit D at deallocation
EXREFERENCE	CHAR(1)	Not used.
EXSTRUCTURE	CHAR(1)	Not used.
EXCOST	CHAR(1)	Not used.
EXPLAN	CHAR(1)	Whether the plan was bound with EXPLAIN YES: N no Y yes
EXPREDICATE	CHAR(1)	Not used.

*Plans are divided into *sections*. The base section of the plan must be in the EDM pool during the entire time the application program is executing. Other sections of the plan, corresponding roughly to sets of related SQL statements, are brought into the pool as needed.

SYSIBM.SYSPLANAUTH Table

The SYSIBM.SYSPLANAUTH table records the privileges held by users for application plans.

Column name	Data type	Description
GRANTOR	CHAR(8)	Authorization ID of the user who granted the privileges.
GRANTEE	CHAR(8)	Authorization ID of the user who holds the privileges or name of a plan that uses the privileges.
NAME	CHAR(8)	Name of the application plan on which the privileges are held.
TIMESTAMP	CHAR(12)	Time at which the privileges were granted (internal time stamp format).
DATEGRANTED	CHAR(6)	Date the privileges were granted; in the form yymmdd.

Column name	Data type	Description
TIMEGRANTED	CHAR(8)	Time the privileges were granted; in the form hhmmssth.
GRANTEETYPE	CHAR(1)	Meaning: blank GRANTEE is an authorization ID P GRANTEE is an application plan
AUTHHOWGOT	CHAR(1)	Authorization level of the user from whom the privileges were received: blank not applicable C DBCTL D DBADM M DBMAINT S SYSADM
BINDAUTH	CHAR(1)	Whether the GRANTEE can use the BIND, REBIND, or FREE commands against the plan: blank privilege is not held G privilege is held with the GRANT option Y privilege is held without the GRANT option
EXECUTEAUTH	CHAR(1)	Whether the GRANTEE can run programs that use the application plan: blank privilege is not held G privilege is held with the GRANT option Y privilege is held without the GRANT option
IBMREQD	CHAR(1)	Whether the row came from the basic machine-readable material (MRM) tape: N no Y yes

SYSIBM.SYSPLANDEP Table

The SYSIBM.SYSPLANDEP table records the dependencies of plans on tables, views, synonyms, table spaces, and indexes.

Column name	Data type	Description
BNAME	VARCHAR(18)	Unqualified name of an object on which the plan is dependent.
BCREATOR	CHAR(8)	If BNAME is a table space, its database. Otherwise, the authorization ID of the creator of BNAME.
BTYPE	CHAR(1)	Type of object BNAME:

Column name	Data type	Description
		I index R table space S synonym T table V view
DNAME	CHAR(8)	Name of the plan.
IBMREQD	CHAR(1)	Whether the row came from the basic machine-readable material (MRM) tape: N no Y yes

SYSIBM.SYSRELS Table

The SYSIBM.SYSRELS table contains one row for every link.

Column name	Data type	Description
CREATOR	CHAR(8)	Authorization ID of the creator of the child table of the link.
TBNAME	VARCHAR(18)	Unqualified name of the child table.
RELNAME	CHAR(8)	Unqualified name of the link.
REFTBNAME	VARCHAR(18)	Unqualified name of the parent table of the link.
REFTBCREATOR	CHAR(8)	Authorization ID of the creator of the parent table.
COLCOUNT	SMALLINT	Number of columns in the foreign key.
DELETERULE	CHAR(1)	Type of delete rule for the link: L CASCADES R RESTRICTED
IBMREQD	CHAR(1)	Whether the row came from the basic machine-readable material (MRM) tape: N no Y yes

SYSIBM.SYSRESAUTH Table

The SYSIBM.SYSRESAUTH table records the privileges held by users over buffer pools, storage groups, and table spaces.

Column name	Data type	Description
GRANTOR	CHAR(8)	Authorization ID of the user who granted the privilege.
GRANTEE	CHAR(8)	Authorization ID of the user who holds the privilege or name of an application plan that uses the privilege.
QUALIFIER	CHAR(8)	This column contains blanks if the row describes a privilege over a buffer pool or storage group. It contains the qualifier of the table space name (the database name), if the row describes a privilege over a table space.
NAME	CHAR(8)	Name of the storage group, table space, or buffer pool.
GRANTEETYPE	CHAR(1)	Meaning: blank GRANTEE is an authorization ID P GRANTEE is an application plan
AUTHHOWGOT	CHAR(1)	Authorization level of the user from whom the privileges were received: blank not applicable C DBCTL D DBADM M DBMAINT S SYSADM
OBTYPE	CHAR(1)	Object type: B buffer pool S storage group R table space
TIMESTAMP	CHAR(12)	Time at which the privilege was granted (internal time stamp format).
DATEGRANTED	CHAR(6)	Date the privilege was granted; in the form yymmdd.
TIMEGRANTED	CHAR(8)	Time the privilege was granted; in the form hhmmssth.
USEAUTH	CHAR(1)	Whether the privilege is held with the GRANT option: G the privilege is held with the GRANT option Y the privilege is held without the GRANT option

Column name	Data type	Description
IBMREQD	CHAR(1)	Whether the row came from the basic machine-readable material (MRM) tape: N no Y yes

SYSIBM.SYSSTMT Table

The SYSIBM.SYSSTMT table contains one or more rows for each SQL statement of each DBRM.

Column name	Data type	Description
NAME	CHAR(8)	Name of the DBRM.
PLNAME	CHAR(8)	Name of the application plan.
PLCREATOR	CHAR(8)	Authorization ID of the creator of the application plan.
SEQNO	SMALLINT	The sequence number of this row; the first portion of the SQL text is stored on row 1 and successive rows have increasing values for SEQNO.
STMTNO	SMALLINT	Statement number of the SQL statement in the source program.
SECTNO	SMALLINT	The number of the plan section containing the SQL statement.
IBMREQD	CHAR(1)	Whether the row came from the basic machine-readable material (MRM) tape: N no Y yes
TEXT	VARCHAR(254)	The text or portion of the text of the SQL statements.

SYSIBM.SYSSTOGROUP Table

The SYSIBM.SYSSTOGROUP table contains one row for each storage group.

Column name	Data type	Description
NAME	CHAR(8)	Name of the storage group.
CREATOR	CHAR(8)	Authorization ID of the creator of the storage group.
VCATNAME	CHAR(8)	Name of the VSAM catalog.

Column name	Data type	Description
VPASSWORD	CHAR(8)	Password for the VSAM catalog.
SPACE	INTEGER	Number of kilobytes of DASD storage allocated to the storage group as determined by the last execution of the STOSPACE utility.
SPCDATE	CHAR(5)	Date when the SPACE column was last updated, in the form yyddd.
IBMREQD	CHAR(1)	Whether the row came from the basic machine-readable material (MRM) tape: N no Y yes

SYSIBM.SYSSYNONYMS Table

The SYSIBM.SYSSYNONYMS table contains one row for each synonym of a table or view.

Column name	Data type	Description
NAME	VARCHAR(18)	Synonym for the table or view.
CREATOR	CHAR(8)	Authorization ID of the creator of the synonym.
TBNAME	VARCHAR(18)	Name of the table or view.
TBCREATOR	CHAR(8)	Authorization ID of the creator of the table or view.
IBMREQD	CHAR(1)	Whether the row came from the basic machine-readable material (MRM) tape: N no Y yes

SYSIBM.SYSTABAUTH Table

The SYSIBM.SYSTABAUTH table records the privileges held by users on tables and views.

Column name	Data type	Description
GRANTOR	CHAR(8)	Authorization ID of the user who granted the privileges.
GRANTEE	CHAR(8)	Authorization ID of the user who holds the privileges or the name of a plan that uses the privileges.
GRANTEETYPE	CHAR(1)	Meaning:

Column name	Data type	Description
		blank GRANTEE is an authorization ID P GRANTEE is an application plan
DBNAME	CHAR(8)	If the privileges were received from a user with DBADM, DBCTRL, or DBMAINT authority, DBNAME is the name of the database on which the GRANTOR has that authority. Otherwise, DBNAME is blank.
SCREATOR	CHAR(8)	If the row of SYSIBM.SYSTABAUTH was created as a result of a CREATE VIEW statement, SCREATOR is the authorization ID of the creator of a table or view referenced in the CREATE VIEW statement. Otherwise, SCREATOR is the same as TCREATOR.
STNAME	VARCHAR(18)	If the row of SYSIBM.SYSTABAUTH was created as a result of a CREATE VIEW statement, STNAME is the name of a table or view referenced in the CREATE VIEW statement. Otherwise, STNAME is the same as TTNAME.
TCREATOR	CHAR(8)	Authorization ID of the creator of the table or view.
TTNAME	VARCHAR(18)	Name of the table or view.
AUTHHOWGOT	CHAR(1)	Authorization level of the user from whom the privileges were received: blank not applicable S SYSADM D DBADM C DBCTL M DBMAINT
TIMESTAMP	CHAR(12)	Time at which the privileges were granted (internal time stamp format).
DATEGRANTED	CHAR(6)	Date the privileges were granted, in the form yymmdd.
TIMEGRANTED	CHAR(8)	Time the privileges were granted, in the form hhmmssth.

Column name	Data type	Description
UPDATECOLS	CHAR(1)	The value of this column is blank if the value of UPDATEAUTH applies uniformly to all columns of the table or view. The value is an asterisk (*) if the value of UPDATEAUTH applies to some columns but not to others. In this case, rows will exist in SYSIBM. SYSCOLAUTH with matching time stamps which list the columns on which update privileges have been granted.
ALTERAUTH	CHAR(1)	Whether the GRANTEE can alter the table: blank privilege not held G privilege is held with the GRANT option Y privilege is held without the GRANT option
DELETEAUTH	CHAR(1)	Whether the GRANTEE can delete rows from the table or view: blank not applicable or privilege not held G privilege is held with the GRANT option Y privilege is held without the GRANT option
INDEXAUTH	CHAR(1)	Whether the GRANTEE can create indexes on the table: blank not applicable or privilege not held G privilege is held with the GRANT option Y privilege is held without the GRANT option
INSERTAUTH	CHAR(1)	Whether the GRANTEE can insert rows into the table or view: blank privilege not held G privilege is held with the GRANT option Y privilege is held without the GRANT option
SELECTAUTH	CHAR(1)	Whether the GRANTEE can select rows from the table or view: blank privilege not held G privilege is held with the GRANT option

Column name	Data type	Description
		Y privilege is held without the GRANT option
UPDATEAUTH	CHAR(1)	Whether the GRANTEE can update rows of the table or view: blank privilege not held G privilege is held with the GRANT option Y privilege is held without the GRANT option
IBMREQD	CHAR(1)	Whether the row came from the basic machine-readable material (MRM) tape: N no Y yes

SYSIBM.SYSTABLEPART Table

The SYSIBM.SYSTABLEPART table contains one row for each unpartitioned table space and one row for each partition of a partitioned table space.

Column name	Data type	Description
PARTITION	SMALLINT	Partition number; 0 if table space is not partitioned.
TSNAME	CHAR(8)	Name of the table space.
DBNAME	CHAR(8)	Name of the database containing the table space.
IXNAME	VARCHAR(18)	Name of the partitioned index. This column is blank if the table space is not partitioned.
IXCREATOR	CHAR(8)	Authorization ID of the creator of the index. This column is blank if the table space is not partitioned.
PQTY	INTEGER	Primary space allocation in units of 4K-byte storage blocks. The value of this column is 0 if a storage group is not used.
SQTY	SMALLINT	Secondary space allocation in units of 4K-byte blocks. The value of this column is 0 if a storage group is not used.
STORTYPE	CHAR(1)	Type of storage allocation: E explicit (storage group not used) I implicit (storage group used)

Column name	Data type	Description
STORNAME	CHAR(8)	Name of storage group used for space allocation. Blank if storage group not used.
VCATNAME	CHAR(8)	Name of VSAM catalog used for space allocation.
CARD	INTEGER	Number of rows in the table space or partition. -1 if statistics not gathered.
FARINDREF	INTEGER	Number of rows that have been relocated far from their original page. -1 if statistics not gathered.
NEARINDREF	INTEGER	Number of rows that have been relocated near their original page. -1 if statistics not gathered.
PERCACTIVE	SMALLINT	Percentage of space occupied by rows of data from active tables. -1 if statistics not gathered.
PERCDROP	SMALLINT	Percentage of space occupied by rows of dropped tables. -1 if statistics have not been gathered.
IBMREQD	CHAR(1)	Whether the row came from the basic machine-readable material (MRM) tape: N no Y yes
LIMITKEY	VARCHAR(512)	Limit key of the partition. 0 if the table space is not partitioned.
FREEPAGE	SMALLINT	The number of pages loaded before a page is left as free space.
PCTFREE	SMALLINT	The percentage of each page left as free space.

SYSIBM.SYSTABLES Table

The SYSIBM.SYSTABLES table contains one row for each table and view.

Column name	Data type	Description
NAME	VARCHAR(18)	Name of the table or view.
CREATOR	CHAR(8)	Authorization ID of the creator of the table or view.
TYPE	CHAR(1)	Whether the row describes a table or view: T table V view

Column name	Data type	Description
DBNAME	CHAR(8)	For a table, or a view of tables, the name of the database that contains the table space named in TSNAME. For a view of a view, the value is DSNDB06.
TSNAME	CHAR(8)	For a table, or a view of one table, the name of the table space that contains the table. For a view of more than one table, the name of a table space that contains one of the tables. For a view of a view, the value is SYSVIEWS.
DBID	SMALLINT	Internal identifier of the database; 0 if the row describes a view.
OBID	SMALLINT	Internal identifier of the table; 0 if the row describes a view.
COLCOUNT	SMALLINT	Number of columns in the table or view.
EDPROC	CHAR(8)	Name of the edit procedure; blank if the row describes a view or a table without an edit procedure.
VALPROC	CHAR(8)	Name of the validation procedure; blank if the row describes a view or a table without a validation procedure.
CLUSTERTYPE	CHAR(1)	Not used; all values are blank.
CLUSTERRID	INTEGER	Not used; all values are 0.
CARD	INTEGER	Total number of rows in the table. -1 if statistics not gathered or the row describes a view. If the table is a catalog table, the value represents a "typical catalog."
NPAGES	INTEGER	Total number of pages on which rows of the table appear. -1 if statistics not gathered or the row describes a view. If the table is a catalog table, the value represents a "typical catalog."
PCTPAGES	SMALLINT	Percentage of total pages of the table space which contain rows of the table. -1 if statistics not gathered or the row describes a view. If the table is a catalog table, the value represents a "typical catalog."

Column name	Data type	Description
IBMREQD	CHAR(1)	Whether the row came from the basic machine-readable material (MRM) tape: N no Y yes
REMARKS	VARCHAR(254)	A character string provided by the user with the COMMENT statement.
PARENTS	SMALLINT	The number of links in which the table is a child.
CHILDREN	SMALLINT	The number of links in which the table is a parent.
KEYCOLUMNS	SMALLINT	The number of columns in the table's primary key.
RECLENGTH	SMALLINT	The maximum length of any record in the table, including all control fields.
STATUS	CHAR(1)	Reserved for future use; all values are blank.
KEYOBID	SMALLINT	Internal DB2 identifier of the index or link that enforces uniqueness of the table's primary key; 0 if not applicable. Not used for user tables.
LABEL	VARCHAR(30)	The table's label as given by a LABEL ON statement; otherwise, an empty string.

SYSIBM.SYSTABLESPACE Table

The SYSIBM.SYSTABLESPACE table contains one row for each table space.

Column name	Data type	Description
NAME	CHAR(8)	Name of the table space.
CREATOR	CHAR(8)	Authorization ID of the creator of the table space.
DBNAME	CHAR(8)	Name of the database.
DBID	SMALLINT	Internal identifier of the database which contains the table space.
OBID	SMALLINT	Internal identifier of the table space file descriptor.
PSID	SMALLINT	Internal identifier of the table space.
BPOOL	CHAR(8)	Name of the buffer pool used for the table space.

Column name	Data type	Description
PARTITIONS	SMALLINT	Number of partitions of the table space; 0 if the table space is not partitioned.
LOCKRULE	CHAR(1)	Lock size of the table space: A any P page S table space
PGSIZE	SMALLINT	Size of pages in the table space in kilobytes.
ERASERULE	CHAR(1)	Whether the data sets are to be erased when dropped. The value is meaningless if the table space is partitioned. N no erase Y erase
STATUS	CHAR(1)	Availability status of the table space: A available C definition is incomplete because no partitioned index has been created T definition is incomplete because no table has been created
IMPLICIT	CHAR(1)	Whether the table space was created implicitly: Y yes N no
NTABLES	SMALLINT	Number of tables defined in the table space.
NACTIVE	INTEGER	Number of active pages in the table space. 0 if statistics are not gathered. If the space is a catalog table space, the value represents a "typical catalog."
DSETPASS	CHAR(8)	The password for the data sets of the table space.
CLOSERULE	CHAR(1)	Whether the data sets are to be closed when the table space is not in use: Y yes N no
SPACE	INTEGER	Number of kilobytes of DASD storage allocated to the table space, as determined by the last execution of the STOSPACE utility. 0 if the table space is not related to a storage group.
IBMREQD	CHAR(1)	Whether the row came from the basic machine-readable material (MRM) tape: N no Y yes

Column name	Data type	Description
ROOTNAME	VARCHAR(18)	Unqualified name of the root table of the space. Blank if it is not a structured table space.
ROOTCREATOR	CHAR(8)	Authorization ID of the creator of the root table. Blank if it is not a structured table space.

SYSIBM.SYSUSERAUTH Table

The SYSIBM.SYSUSERAUTH table records the system privileges held by users.

Column name	Data type	Description
GRANTOR	CHAR(8)	Authorization ID of the user who granted the privileges.
GRANTEE	CHAR(8)	Authorization ID of the user who holds the privileges or the name of a plan that uses the privileges.
TIMESTAMP	CHAR(12)	Time at which the privileges were granted (internal time stamp format).
DATEGRANTED	CHAR(6)	Date the privileges were granted; in the form yymmdd.
TIMEGRANTED	CHAR(8)	Time the privileges were granted; in the form hhmmssth.
GRANTEETYPE	CHAR(1)	Meaning: blank GRANTEE is an authorization ID P GRANTEE is an application plan
AUTHHOWGOT	CHAR(1)	Authorization level of the user from whom the privileges were received: blank not applicable S SYSADM D DBADM C DBCTL M DBMAINT
ALTERBPAUTH	CHAR(1)	This column is not used.
BINDADDAUTH	CHAR(1)	Whether the GRANTEE can use the BIND command with the ADD option: blank authority is not held G privilege is held with the GRANT option Y privilege is held without the GRANT option

Column name	Data type	Description
BSDSAUTH	CHAR(1)	Whether the GRANTEE can issue the -RECOVER BSDS command: blank privilege is not held G privilege is held with the GRANT option Y privilege is held without the GRANT option
CREATEDBAAUTH	CHAR(1)	Whether the GRANTEE can create databases and automatically receive DBADM authority over the new databases: blank authority is not held G authority is held with the GRANT option Y privilege is held without the GRANT option
CREATEDBCAUTH	CHAR(1)	Whether the GRANTEE can create new databases and automatically receive DBCTRL authority over the new databases: blank authority is not held G authority is held with the GRANT option Y authority is held without the GRANT option
CREATESGAUTH	CHAR(1)	Whether the GRANTEE can create new storage groups: blank privilege is not held G privilege is held with the GRANT option Y privilege is held without the GRANT option
DISPLAYAUTH	CHAR(1)	Whether the GRANTEE can use the -DISPLAY commands: blank privilege is not held G privilege is held with the GRANT option Y privilege is held without the GRANT option
RECOVERAUTH	CHAR(1)	Whether the GRANTEE can use the -RECOVER INDOUBT command: G privilege is held with the GRANT option Y privilege is held without the GRANT option
STOPALLAUTH	CHAR(1)	Whether the GRANTEE can use the DB2 -STOP command: blank privilege is not held G privilege is held with the GRANT option

Column name	Data type	Description
		Y privilege is held without the GRANT option
STOSPACEAUTH	CHAR(1)	Whether the GRANTEE can use the STOSPACE utility: blank privilege is not held G privilege is held with the GRANT option Y privilege is held without the GRANT option
SYSADMAUTH	CHAR(1)	Whether the GRANTEE has system administration authority: blank authority is not held G authority is held with the GRANT option Y authority is held without the GRANT option
SYSOPRAUTH	CHAR(1)	Whether the GRANTEE has system operator authority: blank authority is not held G authority is held with the GRANT option Y authority is held without the GRANT option
TRACEAUTH	CHAR(1)	Whether the GRANTEE can issue the -START TRACE and -STOP TRACE commands: blank privilege is not held G privilege is held with the GRANT option Y privilege is held without the GRANT option
IBMREQD	CHAR(1)	Whether the row came from the basic machine-readable material (MRM) tape: N no Y yes

SYSIBM.SYSVIEWDEP Table

The SYSIBM.SYSVIEWDEP table records the dependencies of views on tables and other views.

Column name	Data type	Description
BNAME	VARCHAR(18)	Unqualified name of a table or view on which the view is dependent.
BCREATOR	CHAR(8)	Authorization ID of the creator of BNAME.

Column name	Data type	Description
BTYPE	CHAR(1)	Type of object BNAME: T table V view
DNAME	VARCHAR(18)	Unqualified name of the view.
DCREATOR	CHAR(8)	Authorization ID of the creator of the view.
IBMREQD	CHAR(1)	Whether the row came from the basic machine-readable material (MRM) tape: N no Y yes

SYSIBM.SYSVIEWS Table

The SYSIBM.SYSVIEWS table contains one or more rows for each view.

Column name	Data type	Description
NAME	VARCHAR(18)	Name of the view.
CREATOR	CHAR(8)	Authorization ID of the creator of the view.
SEQNO	SMALLINT	Sequence number of this row; the first portion of the view is on row 1 and successive rows have increasing values of SEQNO.
CHECK	CHAR(1)	Whether the CHECK option was specified in the CREATE VIEW statement: N no Y yes
IBMREQD	CHAR(1)	Whether the row came from the basic machine-readable material (MRM) tape: N no Y yes
TEXT	VARCHAR(254)	The text or portion of the text of the CREATE VIEW statement.

SYSIBM.SYSVLTREE Table

The SYSIBM.SYSVLTREE table contains the remaining part, if any, of the parse tree representation of views.

Column name	Data type	Description
IBMREQD	CHAR(1)	Whether the row came from the basic machine-readable material (MRM) tape: N no Y yes
VTREE	VARCHAR(4000)	The remaining part of the parse tree of a view.

SYSIBM.SYSVOLUMES Table

The SYSIBM.SYSVOLUMES table contains one row for each volume of each storage group.

Column name	Data type	Description
SGNAME	CHAR(8)	The name of the storage group.
SGCREATOR	CHAR(8)	Authorization ID of the creator of the storage group.
VOLID	CHAR(6)	The serial number of the volume.
IBMREQD	CHAR(1)	Whether the row came from the basic machine-readable material (MRM) tape: N no Y yes

SYSIBM.SYSVTREE Table

The SYSIBM.SYSVTREE table contains a row for each view. Each row contains the parse tree of the view. If the parse tree is longer than 4000 bytes, the rest of the parse tree is saved in the SYSIBM.SYSVLTREE table.

Column name	Data type	Description
NAME	VARCHAR(18)	Name of the view.
CREATOR	CHAR(8)	Authorization ID of the creator of the view.
TOTLEN	INTEGER	Total length of the parse tree.
IBMREQD	CHAR(1)	Whether the row came from the basic machine-readable material (MRM) tape: N no Y yes
VTREE	VARCHAR(4000)	Parse tree or portion of the parse tree of the view.

PL/1 CODING EXAMPLES

```
SAMPLE1:PROC OPTIONS(MAIN);                                              00000100
                                                                        00000200
/***********************************************************************/ 00000300
/*                                                                    */ 00000400
/*   THIS PROGRAM READS AN INPUT FILE CONTAINING PATIENT              */ 00000500
/*   IDENTIFICATION NUMBERS AND PRINTS OUT THE PATIENT NAME, ADDRESS  */ 00000600
/*   AND SOCIAL SECURITY NUMBER.                                      */ 00000700
/*                                                                    */ 00000800
/*   AUTHOR: V. TRAN.                                                 */ 00000900
/*                                                                    */ 00001000
/*                                                                    */ 00001100
/***********************************************************************/ 00001200
                                                                        00001300
DCL  IDFILE  FILE RECORD INPUT;                                         00001400
DCL  OUTFILE FILE RECORD OUTPUT;                                        00001500
                                                                        00001600
DCL  01 ID_REC,                                                         00001700
        03 IDNUM                 CHAR(4),                               00001800
        03 FILLER                CHAR(76);                              00001900
                                                                        00002000
DCL  01 PATINFO.                                                        00002100
        03 NAME                  CHAR(10) VARYING,                      00002200
        03 ID                    CHAR(4),                               00002300
        03 ADDRESS               CHAR(30) VARYING,                      00002400
        03 BIRTHDATE             CHAR(6),                               00002500
        03 SEX                   CHAR(1),                               00002600
        03 SOCSEC                CHAR(9);                               00002700
                                                                        00002800
DCL EOF                          BIT(1) INIT('0'B),                     00002900
    LYNES                        FIXED BIN(31) INIT(99),                00003000
    SUBSTR                       BUILTIN;                               00003100
                                                                        00003200
DCL 01 HDR1,                                                            00003300
        03 CNTL1                 CHAR(1)  INIT('1'),                    00003400
        03 FILLR1                CHAR(12) INIT                          00003500
                                   ('PATIENT NAME'),                    00003600
        03 FILLR2                CHAR(5)  INIT(' '),                    00003700
        03 FILLR3                CHAR(10) INIT                          00003800
                                   ('PATIENT ID'),                     00003900
        03 FILLR4                CHAR(5)  INIT(' '),                    00004000
        03 FILLR5                CHAR(30) INIT                          00004100
                                   ('ADDRESS                    '),00004200
        03 FILLR6                CHAR(5)  INIT(' '),                    00004300
        03 FILLR7                CHAR(22) INIT                          00004400
                                   ('SOCIAL SECURITY NUMBER'),          00004500
        03 FILLR8                CHAR(43) INIT(' ');                    00004600
                                                                        00004700
DCL 01 HDR2,                                                            00004800
        03 CNTL2                 CHAR(1)  INIT(' '),                    00004900
        03 FILLR1                CHAR(12) INIT                          00005000
                                   ('------------'),                    00005100
        03 FILLR2                CHAR(5)  INIT(' '),                    00005200
        03 FILLR3                CHAR(10) INIT                          00005300
                                   ('----------'),                      00005400
        03 FILLR4                CHAR(5)  INIT(' '),                    00005500
        03 FILLR5                CHAR(30) INIT                          00005600
                                   ('------------------------------'),00005700
        03 FILLR6                CHAR(5)  INIT(' '),                    00005800
        03 FILLR7                CHAR(22) INIT                          00005900
                                   ('----------------------'),          00006000
```

Fig. B.1 PATIENT table retrieval program.

```
          03 FILLR8                   CHAR(43) INIT(' ');            00006100
                                                                    00006200
DCL 01 DETAIL,                                                      00006300
          03 CNTL                     CHAR(1)  INIT(' '),           00006400
          03 RP_NAME                  CHAR(10),                     00006500
          03 FILLR1                   CHAR(7)  INIT(' '),           00006600
          03 RP_ID                    CHAR(4),                      00006700
          03 FILLR2                   CHAR(11) INIT(' '),           00006800
          03 RP_ADDRESS               CHAR(30),                     00006900
          03 FILLR3                   CHAR(5)  INIT(' '),           00007000
          03 RP_SOC_SEC               CHAR(11),                     00007100
          03 FILLR4                   CHAR(54) INIT(' ');           00007200
                                                                    00007300
EXEC SQL DECLARE PATIENT TABLE                                      00007400
          (PATNAME        VARCHAR(10)  NOT NULL,                    00007500
           PATNO          CHAR(4)      NOT NULL,                    00007600
           ADDRESS        VARCHAR(30),                              00007700
           BIRTHDATE      CHAR(6),                                  00007800
           SEX            CHAR(1),                                  00007900
           SSNUM          CHAR(9)      NOT NULL WITH DEFAULT);      00008000
                                                                    00008100
EXEC SQL INCLUDE SQLCA;                                             00008200
                                                                    00008300
OPEN FILE (IDFILE)   INPUT,                                         00008400
     FILE (OUTFILE) OUTPUT;                                         00008500
ON ENDFILE (IDFILE) EOF = '1'B;                                     00008600
                                                                    00008700
CALL PRT_HEADING;                                                   00008800
READ FILE (IDFILE) INTO(ID_REC);                                    00008900
                                                                    00009000
DO WHILE (¬ EOF);                                                   00009100
   EXEC SQL SELECT *                                                00009200
            INTO :PATINFO                                           00009300
            FROM PATIENT                                            00009400
            WHERE PATNO = :IDNUM;                                   00009500
                                                                    00009600
   IF SQLCODE = 0 THEN                                              00009700
      CALL PRT_DETAIL;                                              00009800
                                                                    00009900
   READ FILE (IDFILE) INTO(ID_REC);                                 00010000
                                                                    00010100
END;                                                                00010200
                                                                    00010300
CLOSE FILE (IDFILE), FILE (OUTFILE);                                00010400
                                                                    00010500
PRT_HEADING:                                                        00010600
   PROCEDURE;                                                       00010700
                                                                    00010800
      WRITE FILE (OUTFILE) FROM (HDR1);                             00010900
      WRITE FILE (OUTFILE) FROM (HDR2);                             00011000
      LYNES = 2;                                                    00011100
                                                                    00011200
   END PRT_HEADING;                                                 00011300
                                                                    00011400
PRT_DETAIL:                                                         00011500
   PROCEDURE;                                                       00011600
                                                                    00011700
      RP_NAME    = NAME;                                            00011800
      RP_ID      = ID;                                              00011900
      RP_ADDRESS = ADDRESS;                                         00012000
                                                                    00012000
      RP_SOC_SEC = SUBSTR(SOCSEC,1,3) || '-' || SUBSTR(SOCSEC,4,2) ||  00012100
                   '-' || SUBSTR(SOCSEC,6,4);                       00012200
                                                                    00012300
      IF LYNES > 57 THEN DO;                                        00012400
         LYNES = 0;                                                 00012500
         CALL PRT_HEADING;                                          00012600
      END;                                                          00012700
                                                                    00012800
      LYNES = LYNES + 1;                                            00012900
      WRITE FILE (OUTFILE) FROM (DETAIL);                           00013000
                                                                    00013100
      NAME    = ' ';                                                00013200
      ADDRESS = ' ';                                                00013300
                                                                    00013400
   END PRT_DETAIL;                                                  00013500
                                                                    00013600
END SAMPLE1;                                                        00013700
```

Fig. B.1 *(Continued)*

```
SAMPLE2:PROC OPTIONS(MAIN);                                              00000100
                                                                        00000200
/**********************************************************************/ 00000300
/*                                                                 */    00000400
/*    THIS PROGRAM READS AN INPUT FILE CONTAINING PATIENT          */    00000500
/*    IDENTIFICATION NUMBERS AND PRINTS OUT THE INFORMATION FOR    */    00000600
/*    EACH PATIENT VISIT.                                          */    00000700
/*                                                                 */    00000800
/*    AUTHOR:  V. TRAN.                                            */    00000900
/*                                                                 */    00001000
/*                                                                 */    00001100
/**********************************************************************/ 00001200
                                                                        00001300
DCL   IDFILE   FILE RECORD INPUT;                                       00001400
DCL   OUTFILE FILE RECORD OUTPUT;                                       00001500
                                                                        00001600
DCL  01 ID_REC,                                                         00001700
         05 IDNUM                 CHAR(4),                              00001800
         05 FILLER                CHAR(76);                             00001900
                                                                        00002000
DCL  01 VISITINFO,                                                      00002100
         03 ID                    CHAR(4),                              00002200
         03 SEQUENCE              CHAR(3),                              00002300
         03 MDNO                  CHAR(3),                              00002400
         03 ADDATE                CHAR(6),                              00002500
         03 DSDATE                CHAR(6),                              00002600
         03 DIAGNOSIS             CHAR(20) VARYING;                     00002700
                                                                        00002800
DCL EOF                           BIT(1) INIT('0'B),                   00002900
    LYNES                         FIXED BIN(31) INIT(99),              00003000
    MORE_RECORD                   BIT(1);                               00003100
                                                                        00003200
DCL 01 HDR1,                                                            00003300
        03 CNTL1                  CHAR(1)  INIT('1'),                   00003400
        03 FILLR1                 CHAR(10) INIT                         00003500
                                    ('PATIENT ID'),                     00003600
        03 FILLR2                 CHAR(3)  INIT(' '),                   00003700
        03 FILLR3                 CHAR(10) INIT                         00003800
                                    ('SEQUENCE   '),                    00003900
        03 FILLR4                 CHAR(3)  INIT(' '),                   00004000
        03 FILLR5                 CHAR(10) INIT                         00004100
                                    ('PHYSICIAN '),                     00004200
        03 FILLR6                 CHAR(3)  INIT(' '),                   00004300
        03 FILLR7                 CHAR(10) INIT                         00004400
                                    ('ADMIT DATE'),                     00004500
        03 FILLR8                 CHAR(3)  INIT(' '),                   00004600
        03 FILLR9                 CHAR(10) INIT                         00004700
                                    ('DSCH. DATE'),                     00004800
        03 FILLR10                CHAR(3)  INIT(' '),                   00004900
        03 FILLR11                CHAR(20) INIT                         00005000
                                    ('DIAGNOSIS            '),          00005100
        03 FILLR12                CHAR(47) INIT(' ');                   00005200
                                                                        00005300
DCL 01 HDR2,                                                            00005400
        03 CNTL2                  CHAR(1)  INIT(' '),                   00005500
        03 FILLR1                 CHAR(10) INIT                         00005600
                                    ('----------'),                     00005700
        03 FILLR2                 CHAR(3)  INIT(' '),                   00005800
        03 FILLR3                 CHAR(10) INIT                         00005900
                                    ('----------'),                     00006000
```

Fig. B.2 VISIT table retrieval program.

```
          03 FILLR4              CHAR(3)  INIT(' '),          00006100
          03 FILLR5              CHAR(10) INIT                00006200
                                   ('----------'),           00006300
          03 FILLR6              CHAR(3)  INIT(' '),          00006400
          03 FILLR7              CHAR(10) INIT                00006500
                                   ('----------'),           00006600
          03 FILLR8              CHAR(3)  INIT(' '),          00006700
          03 FILLR9              CHAR(10) INIT                00006800
                                   ('----------'),           00006900
          03 FILLR10             CHAR(3)  INIT(' '),          00007000
          03 FILLR11             CHAR(20) INIT                00007100
                                   ('-----+----------------'), 00007200
          03 FILLR12             CHAR(47) INIT(' ');          00007300
                                                             00007400
DCL 01 DETAIL,                                               00007500
          03 CNTL               CHAR(1)  INIT(' '),          00007600
          03 RP_ID              CHAR(4),                     00007700
          03 FILLR1             CHAR(9)  INIT(' '),          00007800
          03 RP_SEQ             CHAR(3),                     00007900
          03 FILLR2             CHAR(10) INIT(' '),          00008000
          03 RP_PHYSICIAN       CHAR(3),                     00008100
          03 FILLR3             CHAR(10) INIT(' '),          00008200
          03 RP_ADMIT           CHAR(6),                     00008300
          03 FILLR4             CHAR(7)  INIT(' '),          00008400
          03 RP_DISCH           CHAR(6),                     00008500
          03 FILLR5             CHAR(7)  INIT(' '),          00008600
          03 RP_DIAGNOSIS       CHAR(20),                    00008700
          03 FILLR6             CHAR(47) INIT(' ');          00008800
                                                             00008900
EXEC SQL DECLARE VISIT TABLE                                 00009000
          (IDNO        CHAR(4)      NOT NULL,                00009100
           SEQUN       CHAR(3)      NOT NULL,                00009200
           MDNO        CHAR(3)      NOT NULL,                00009300
           ADDATE      CHAR(6)      NOT NULL,                00009400
           DSDATE      CHAR(6)      ,                        00009500
           DIAGNOSIS   VARCHAR(20)  NOT NULL WITH DEFAULT);  00009600
                                                             00009700
EXEC SQL INCLUDE SQLCA;                                      00009800
                                                             00009900
EXEC SQL DECLARE PVISIT CURSOR FOR                           00010000
          SELECT *                                           00010100
          FROM VISIT                                         00010200
          WHERE IDNO = :IDNUM ;                              00010300
                                                             00010400
OPEN FILE (IDFILE)   INPUT,                                  00010500
     FILE (OUTFILE) OUTPUT;                                  00010600
ON ENDFILE (IDFILE) EOF = '1'B;                              00010700
                                                             00010800
CALL PRT_HEADING;                                            00010900
READ FILE (IDFILE) INTO(ID_REC);                             00011000
                                                             00011100
DO WHILE (¬ EOF);                                            00011200
   EXEC SQL OPEN PVISIT ;                                    00011300
                                                             00011400
   EXEC SQL FETCH PVISIT INTO :VISITINFO ;                   00011500
                                                             00011600
   IF SQLCODE = 0 THEN DO;                                   00011700
      MORE_RECORD = '1'B;                                    00011800
      DO WHILE (MORE_RECORD);                                00011900
         CALL PRT_DETAIL;                                    00012000
```

Fig. B.2   *(Continued)*

```
        EXEC SQL FETCH PVISIT INTO :VISITINFO ;          00012100
        IF SQLCODE ¬ = 0 THEN                            00012200
            MORE_RECORD = '0'B;                          00012300
      END;                                               00012400
   END;                                                  00012500
   EXEC SQL CLOSE PVISIT ;                               00012600
                                                         00012700
   READ FILE (IDFILE) INTO(ID_REC);                      00012800
                                                         00012900
END;                                                     00013000
                                                         00013100
CLOSE FILE (IDFILE), FILE (OUTFILE);                     00013200
                                                         00013300
PRT_HEADING:                                             00013400
   PROCEDURE;                                            00013500
                                                         00013600
      WRITE FILE (OUTFILE) FROM (HDR1);                  00013700
      WRITE FILE (OUTFILE) FROM (HDR2);                  00013800
      LYNES = 2;                                         00013900
                                                         00014000
   END PRT_HEADING;                                      00014100
                                                         00014200
PRT_DETAIL:                                              00014300
   PROCEDURE;                                            00014400
                                                         00014500
      RP_ID        = ID;                                 00014600
      RP_SEQ       = SEQUENCE;                           00014700
      RP_PHYSICIAN = MDNO;                               00014800
      RP_ADMIT     = ADDATE;                             00014900
      RP_DISCH     = DSDATE;                             00015000
      RP_DIAGNOSIS = DIAGNOSIS;                          00015100
                                                         00015200
      IF LYNES > 57 THEN DO;                             00015300
        LYNES = 0;                                       00015400
        CALL PRT_HEADING;                                00015500
      END;                                               00015600
                                                         00015700
      LYNES = LYNES + 1;                                 00015800
      WRITE FILE (OUTFILE) FROM (DETAIL);                00015900
                                                         00016000
      DIAGNOSIS = ' ';                                   00016100
                                                         00016200
   END PRT_DETAIL;                                       00016300
                                                         00016400
END SAMPLE2;                                             00016500
```

Fig. B.2   *(Continued)*

```
SAMPLE3:PROC OPTIONS(MAIN);                                             00000100
                                                                        00000200
/*********************************************************************/ 00000300
/*                                                                */     00000400
/*   THIS PROGRAM READS AN INPUT FILE CONTAINING PATIENT NAME,    */     00000500
/*   IDENTIFICATION NUMBERS, ADDRESS, BIRTHDATE, AND SOCIAL SECURITY */  00000600
/*   NUMBER AND LOADS THE PATIENT TABLE.                          */     00000700
/*                                                                */     00000800
/*   AUTHOR:  V. TRAN.                                            */     00000900
/*                                                                */     00001000
/*                                                                */     00001100
/*********************************************************************/ 00001200
                                                                        00001300
DCL  IDFILE  FILE RECORD INPUT;                                         00001400
DCL  OUTFILE FILE RECORD OUTPUT;                                        00001500
                                                                        00001600
DCL  01 ID_REC,                                                         00001700
        05 IDNUM                 CHAR(4),                               00001800
        05 FILLER                CHAR(76);                              00001900
                                                                        00002000
DCL  01 PATINFO.                                                        00002100
        03 NAME                  CHAR(10) VARYING,                      00002200
        03 ID                    CHAR(4),                               00002300
        03 ADDRESS               CHAR(30) VARYING,                      00002400
        03 BIRTHDATE             CHAR(6),                               00002500
        03 SEX                   CHAR(1),                               00002600
        03 SOCSEC                CHAR(9);                               00002700
                                                                        00002800
DCL EOF                          BIT(1) INIT('0'B),                     00002900
    INREC                        FIXED BIN(15) INIT(0),                 00003000
    OUTREC                       FIXED BIN(15) INIT(0);                 00003100
                                                                        00003200
DCL 01 DETAIL,                                                          00003300
        03 CNTL                  CHAR(1)  INIT(' '),                    00003400
        03 FILLR1                CHAR(5)  INIT(' '),                    00003500
        03 MSSG                  CHAR(30),                              00003600
        03 FILLR2                CHAR(1)  INIT(' '),                    00003700
        03 RCOUNT                PIC '999',                             00003800
        03 FILLR3                CHAR(41) INIT(' ');                    00003900
                                                                        00004000
EXEC SQL DECLARE PATIENT TABLE                                          00004100
          (PATNAME        VARCHAR(10)  NOT NULL,                        00004200
           PATNO          CHAR(4)      NOT NULL,                        00004300
           ADDRESS        VARCHAR(30),                                  00004400
           BIRTHDATE      CHAR(6),                                      00004500
           SEX            CHAR(1),                                      00004600
           SSNUM          CHAR(9)       NOT NULL WITH DEFAULT);         00004700
                                                                        00004800
EXEC SQL INCLUDE SQLCA;                                                 00004900
                                                                        00005000
OPEN FILE (IDFILE)   INPUT,                                             00005100
     FILE (OUTFILE)  OUTPUT;                                            00005200
ON ENDFILE (IDFILE) EOF = '1'B;                                         00005300
                                                                        00005400
READ FILE (IDFILE) INTO(PATINFO);                                       00005500
                                                                        00005600
DO WHILE (¬ EOF);                                                       00005700
    INREC = INREC + 1;                                                  00005800
    EXEC SQL INSERT INTO PATIENT                                        00005900
             VALUES (:PATINFO);                                         00006000

                                                                        00006100
                                                                        00006200
    IF SQLCODE = 0 THEN                                                 00006300
        OUTREC = OUTREC + 1;                                            00006400
                                                                        00006500
    READ FILE (IDFILE) INTO(PATINFO);                                   00006600
                                                                        00006700
END;                                                                    00006800
MSSG    = '***** TOTAL RECORDS READ      :';                            00006900
RCOUNT = INREC;                                                         00007000
WRITE FILE (OUTFILE) FROM (DETAIL);                                     00007100
                                                                        00007200
MSSG    = '***** TOTAL RECORDS INSERTED :';                            00007300
RCOUNT = OUTREC;                                                        00007400
WRITE FILE (OUTFILE) FROM (DETAIL);                                     00007500
                                                                        00007600
CLOSE FILE (IDFILE), FILE (OUTFILE);                                    00007700
                                                                        00007800
END SAMPLE3;
```

Fig. B.3 PATIENT table load program.

```
SAMPLE4:PROC OPTIONS(MAIN);                                         00000100
                                                                    00000200
/*****************************************************************/ 00000300
/*                                                             */   00000400
/*   THIS PROGRAM READS AN INPUT FILE CONTAINING NONSELECT     */   00000500
/*   STATEMENTS AND EXECUTES THEM DYNAMICALLY.  EACH SQL STATEMENT */ 00000600
/*   IS CONTAINED IN ONE RECORD AND DELIMITED BY A SEMICOLON.  */   00000700
/*                                                             */   00000800
/*   AUTHOR:  V. TRAN.                                         */   00000900
/*                                                             */   00001000
/*                                                             */   00001100
/*****************************************************************/ 00001200
DCL  STMTFILE FILE RECORD INPUT;                                    00001300
DCL  OUTFILE  FILE RECORD OUTPUT;                                   00001400
                                                                    00001500
DCL STMT_REC                      CHAR(160) INIT(' ');              00001600
DCL 1 STMT-BUFFER DEFINED STMT_REC POS(1),                          00001700
      03 FIELD1                   CHAR(80),                         00001800
      03 FIELD2                   CHAR(80);                         00001900
                                                                    00002000
DCL STMT_AREA                     CHAR(160) VARYING;                00002100
                                                                    00002200
DCL EOF                           BIT(1) INIT('0'B),                00002300
    LYNES                         FIXED BIN(31) INIT(99),           00002400
    (INREC,OUTC,I)                FIXED BIN(15) INIT(0),            00002500
    (SUBSTR,LENGTH)               BUILTIN;                          00002600
                                                                    00002700
DCL OUTREC                        CHAR(133);                        00002800
DCL 01 DETAIL1 DEFINED OUTREC POS(1),                               00002900
      03 CNTL1                    CHAR(1)  INIT(' '),               00003000
      03 FILLR1                   CHAR(5)  INIT(' '),               00003100
      03 MSSG                     CHAR(30),                         00003200
      03 FILLR2                   CHAR(1)  INIT(' '),               00003300
      03 CODE                     PIC '99999999-',                 00003400
      03 FILLR3                   CHAR(87) INIT(' ');               00003500
                                                                    00003600
DCL 01 DETAIL2 DEFINED OUTREC POS(1),                               00003700
      03 CNTL2                    CHAR(1)  INIT(' '),               00003800
      03 FILLR1                   CHAR(36) INIT(' '),               00003900
      03 DTL_LINE                 CHAR(80) INIT(' '),               00004000
      03 FILLR2                   CHAR(16) INIT(' ');               00004100
                                                                    00004200
EXEC SQL INCLUDE SQLCA;                                             00004300
                                                                    00004400
OPEN FILE (STMTFILE) INPUT,                                         00004500
     FILE (OUTFILE)  OUTPUT;                                        00004600
ON ENDFILE (STMTFILE) EOF = '1'B;                                   00004700
                                                                    00004800
READ FILE (STMTFILE) INTO(STMT_REC);                                00004900
                                                                    00005000
DO WHILE (¬ EOF);                                                   00005100
   INREC    = INREC + 1;                                            00005200
   STMT_AREA = ' ';                                                 00005300
   DO I = LENGTH(STMT_REC) TO 1 BY -1;                              00005400
     IF SUBSTR(STMT_REC,I,1) = ';' THEN LEAVE;                      00005500
   END;                                                             00005600
   STMT_AREA = SUBSTR(STMT_REC,1,I-1);                              00005700
                                                                    00005800
   EXEC SQL EXECUTE IMMEDIATE :STMT_AREA;                           00005900
                                                                    00006000
```

Fig. B.4 Sample dynamic SQL program.

```
        IF SQLCODE = 0 THEN                           00006100
           OUTC = OUTC + 1;                           00006200
        ELSE                                          00006300
           CALL ERR_PRT;                              00006400
                                                      00006500
                                                      00006600
        READ FILE (STMTFILE) INTO(STMT_REC);          00006700
                                                      00006800
                                                      00006900
END;                                                  00007000
OUTREC = ' ';                                         00007100
MSSG   = '***** TOTAL RECORDS READ      :';           00007200
CODE   = INREC;                                       00007300
WRITE FILE (OUTFILE) FROM (OUTREC);                   00007400
                                                      00007500
OUTREC = ' ';                                         00007600
MSSG   = '***** TOTAL RECORDS PROCESSED:';            00007700
CODE   = OUTC;                                        00007800
WRITE FILE (OUTFILE) FROM (OUTREC);                   00007900
                                                      00008000
CLOSE FILE (IDFILE), FILE (STMTFILE);                 00008100
                                                      00008200
ERR_PRT:                                              00008300
   PROCEDURE;                                         00008400
                                                      00008500
      OUTREC = ' ';                                   00008600
      MSSG   = '***** STATEMENT ERROR      :';        00008700
      CODE   = SQLCODE;                               00008800
      CALL WRITE_LINE;                                00008900
                                                      00009000
      OUTREC   = ' ';                                 00009100
      DTL_LINE = FIELD1;                              00009200
      CALL WRITE_LINE;                                00009300
                                                      00009400
      OUTREC   = ' ';                                 00009500
      DTL_LINE = FIELD2;                              00009600
      CALL WRITE_LINE;                                00009700
                                                      00009800
   END ERR_PRT;                                       00009900
                                                      00010000
WRITE_LINE:                                           00010100
   PROCEDURE;                                         00010200
                                                      00010300
      IF LYNES > 57 THEN DO;                          00010400
         LYNES = 0;                                   00010500
         SUBSTR(OUTREC,1,1) = '1';                    00010600
      END;                                            00010700
                                                      00010800
      LYNES = LYNES + 1;                              00010900
      WRITE FILE (OUTFILE) FROM (OUTREC);             00011000
                                                      00011100
   END WRITE_LINE;                                    00011200
                                                      00011300
END SAMPLE4;

Sample Dynamic SQL Program
```

Fig. B.4 *(Continued)*

HOST ALLOWABLE DATA TYPES

The following are the available DB2 data types and their equivalents in Cobol and PL/1 languages.

DB2 Data type	Cobol data type	PL/1 data type
CHAR(n)	01 variable PIC X(n)	DCL variable CHAR(n);
DECIMAL(m,n)	01 variable PIC S9(m)V9(n)COMP-3.	DCL variable FIXED DEC(m,n);
FLOAT	01 variable COMP-2.	DCL variable BIN FLOAT(53);
GRAPHIC(n)	01 variable PIC G(n) DISPLAY-1.	DCL variable GRAPHIC(n);
INTEGER	01 variable PIC S9(n) COMP.	DCL variable FIXED BIN(31);
SMALLINT	01 variable PIC S9(n) COMP.	DCL variable FIXED BIN(15);
VARCHAR(n)	01 variable. 49 variable PIC S9(m) COMP. 49 variable PIC X(n).	DCL variable CHAR(n)VARYING;
VARGRAPHIC(n)	01 variable. 49 variable PIC S9(m) COMP.49 variable PIC G(n) DISPLAY-1.	DCL variable GRAPHIC(n) VARYING;

The following are the explanations of the use of the above DB2 data types in Cobol and PL/1 languages:

For CHAR data type, the integer n should match the length of the CHAR column; n must be from 1 to 254.

For DECIMAL data type, the total number of digits m and the number of digits in the fractional part n must match the column defined as DECIMAL; m cannot be greater than 15.

For GRAPHIC data type, the value of n must be from 1 to 127.

For INTEGER data type, in Cobol the value of n must be an integer from 5 to 9.

For SMALLINT data type, in Cobol the value of n must be an integer from 1 to 4.

For VARCHAR and VARGRAPHIC data types, in Cobol the value of m must be an integer from 1 to 4, and the value of n must match the length of the column defined as VARCHAR or VARGRAPHIC. In PL/1, the value of n must match the maximum length of the column defined as VARCHAR or VARGRAPHIC.

DB2 RESERVED WORDS

The following words are reserved words in SQL. They may not be used as ordinary identifiers in forming names. They may be used as delimited identifiers by enclosing them between double quotation marks.

ADD	DROP	INTO	SET
ALL	EDITPROC	IS	STOGROUP
ALTER	END-EXEC*	LIKE	SYNONYM
AND	ERASE	LOCKSIZE	TABLE
ANY	EXECUTE	NOT	TABLESPACE
AS	EXISTS	NULL	TO
BETWEEN	FIELDPROC	NUMPARTS	UNION
BUFFERPOOL	FOR	PROC	UPDATE
BY	FROM	OF	USER
CLUSTER	GO	ON	USING
COLUMN	GOTO	OR	VALIDPROC
COUNT	GRANT	ORDER	VALUES
CURRENT	GROUP	PART	VCAT
CURSOR	HAVING	PLAN	VIEW
DATABASE	IMMEDIATE	PRIQTY	VOLUMES
DELETE	IN	PRIVILEGES	WHERE
DESCRIPTOR	INDEX	SECQTY	WITH
DISTINCT	INSERT	SELECT	

---

*COBOL only

Index

ABOUT THE AUTHOR

Viet G. Tran is principal programmer for the UCLA Medical Center
Computing Services. He earned his Bachelor's degree in computer science
from UCLA and Master's degree in computer science with an emphasis in
Database Management Systems from West Coast University.